D0121470

Eighteen Moons

Andi Webb

Andi Webb

Published by:

My Life Publishing Limited

www.mylifepublishing.co.uk

80 – 83 Long Lane

London EC1A 9ET

ISBN: 9781739754679

Hardback Edition 2022

Andi Webb

Chapter 1

The Patter of Tiny Paws

'He's adorable!'

'He is. Perfect.'

We looked at one another and grinned as a small bundle of white fur crawled steadily towards us. We had both fallen instantly and totally in love.

We were in the large garden of a house in West Sussex and the two of us were peering over the top of an old-fashioned pigsty on stilts. Inside were twelve perfect white puppies, just a couple of weeks old.

We'd asked the breeder, Mrs Bennett, how many boys there were. 'Just the two,' she'd said, pulling out one pup after another and turning them upside down. When she'd found the two males, she placed them at the opposite end of the pigsty. One began crawling straight back to his sisters while the other, steady, and determined, headed towards us.

We'd found our boy.

We'd agreed on a name before we met him. Remus. And it suited him.

'Come on Remus,' I whispered, as he reached my outstretched hand and was rewarded with a gentle scratch behind his tiny ear.

'By the time you collect him he'll have his spots,' Mrs B said.

Yes, our 'first-born' was a Dalmatian. Known for being a lively and intelligent breed. Also, as we were soon to discover, hyperactive and ferociously needy.

Tearing ourselves away we arranged to pick Remus up in six weeks' time and set off on the two-hour drive home. I was beside myself with excitement, already planning my trip to buy a bed, blankets, toys, and treats for the new addition to our family. John, at the wheel, was quiet, focussing on the road. But I knew he was as happy as I was. We'd waited a long time to make this commitment but now the time felt right, and we both felt good about it.

Both of us in our mid-thirties, we had been a couple for eight years. Buying our London flat after three years had been part of our decision to settle down together, although I think we both knew from the moment we met that we'd stay together. Creating a 'nest' for the two of us was the next step as we made the inevitable transition from being young men partying about town to a couple who preferred quiet dinners a deux or curling up on the sofa and watching a film.

That had been five years earlier. And not long after we put the finishing touches to our flat, we had begun to hanker for the patter of tiny feet or, in our case, paws. We'd put it off because we were both out all day; I was working in clothing design, with a small workshop of my own while John was an accountant. We both worked long hours and we didn't want to leave a dog cooped up at home.

But as time passed, we began to feel seriously broody. This was only made worse when a friend gave us a Disney Dalmatian toy one Christmas. She did say it was probably as close to a real dog as we should get. And we did listen to her, for a bit, but in the end our longing for a real canine to cuddle won over all practical considerations. The flat just didn't feel right without a dog.

Fast forward and here we were, delighted with our boy and counting the days until we could bring him home.

Little did we know that those weeks up to his arrival were the last moments of peace and quiet we would share for quite some time. And that the flat, with its carefully chosen oak floors and antique tables, would soon be a battered shadow of its former self. From the moment we picked him up, Remus, a non-stop whirlwind of high-velocity energy, launched himself into our lives with such face-licking, tail-wagging exuberance that we were both left reeling. He never stopped racing around apart from when he was chewing the furniture, books, CDs, shoes – in fact anything that was chewable and quite a few things that weren't.

He was constantly hungry and constantly demanding attention, co-opting both the sofa and the bed and insisting on endless cuddles, inserting himself between us whenever he felt he wasn't getting his fair dues.

He cost us a fortune in damage, food, and vet bills but despite all of it we adored him. He was lean, strong, glistening white with inky black spots and a handsome head – a showstopper of a dog who got compliments wherever he went. But most of all he was our boy; he had a way of looking up at us with such innocent cheerfulness that we could never stay angry with him for long.

We hired a dog walker to come and take him out for long walks while we were at work. But after a couple of months, she told us she was spending so much on headache tablets because of the stress of managing him that she couldn't walk him any longer. After that we paid a friend to dog sit him, but she didn't even last a month. She couldn't get anything done when he was around, he was all over her, constantly.

Our next dog walkers were a couple. We hoped two people might manage him better than one. But a couple of months on they told us, 'We've just changed our catchment area and you're no longer in it – sorry.'

The lengths people went to in order to avoid having Remus were quite funny. Except that it left us needing to find a way to manage him ourselves. He couldn't go to work with John in the corporate accountancy firm where he worked, so we decided he'd have to come with me to my small studio in Southwark. Each morning we set off for the tube, where Remus entertained fellow passengers by tearing up any newspapers left on seats and spinning in dizzying circles on the platform – earning himself regular applause from laughing tourists.

Needless to say, I didn't get a lot of work done, since I ended up taking him to the park about four times a day to try to tire him out. I met another dog-owner there one day who told me he'd given up on his Dalmatian and given it away. 'Just too needy and energetic mate,' he said, shaking his head at Remus, who was trying to badger a sedate old spaniel into playing with him.

'Tell me about it,' I thought. We knew by this time just how full-on Dalmatians were. Once used as carriage dogs, they are happy to run literally all day long. Sitting about just isn't their thing. But we never once thought of giving Remus away. He was ours and we loved him, uncontrollable wretch or not.

Then, when Remus was three, we compounded our foolish choice of dog by taking on a second one.

I know.

But in our defence, we thought it might calm him down to have a companion.

At two years old we'd listed him on a dog studding website and when a local couple got in touch, we took him along for his first romantic encounter. Things started off a tad shakily, Remus clearly had no experience in the ways of amour and just wanted to play. But he got there eventually, without the use of the electric prod the couple suggested we insert in his nether regions to prompt ejaculation, which I politely declined. A few weeks later a pregnancy was declared, and Remus earned his first wage. 'We'll put that towards some of the repairs,' John muttered to him. 'Not to mention your food bills'.

His third liaison, with a Dalmatian from Essex, produced a litter of pups. The owner suggested we take the pick of the litter as our fee and, thinking we'd sell her, we agreed and picked a bouncy female puppy. We took her home and called her Gracie.

Big mistake that. Once we'd named her, we just couldn't bring ourselves to sell her. And once we realised that we were keeping her, it was inevitable that I start working from home. I couldn't have managed both of them on the commute or in my workshop.

Truth to tell, business wasn't going well. I'd already downsized from my overpriced premises and small staff team to just me in the workshop. I had trained in the garment industry, learning everything from the conception of a garment to pattern cutting and I was still designing my own range, but the recession of the late 90s had bitten hard and by this stage I was only just about covering costs. At the same time John's career was soaring, he'd started his own firm and it was successful from the off. So, I let my workshop go, downsized again to the dining table as my 'office' and, while attempting to do a bit of work, became a more or less full-time dog parent.

Clearly our dog-training skills had not improved one iota. Gracie was, if anything, worse than Remus. She chewed absolutely everything and nothing we tried made any difference. Her speciality was phones. She chomped her way through a Blackberry and an iPhone in her first week alone. Not only that, but she was impossible to house-train, and our solid oak floors were regularly soaked in dog pee. We were horrified, but being two big softies, we couldn't get rid of her, Gracie was ours, just as much as Remus was. They got on extremely well and when they did – finally – settle down at the end of each day it was together, curled comfortably side by side on the sofa. Leaving precious little room for us, of course. But we, with paternal indulgence, simply squeezed ourselves into the remaining few inches of space at either end.

Our two hounds did satisfy our longing to be parents, at least for a while but, perhaps inevitably, our thoughts strayed towards babies – the humankind – and we wondered whether children might ever be a possibility for us.

John came from a big, warm Irish family and while my family set-up was a little more complex than his, we both felt that having children was something we would love.

It was also a promise I had made to my father. When I told him, as a teenager, that 'I might be gay,' there had been a long pause before he said, 'Son, what you are and what you are not, you will figure out in the goodness of time. So be gay, as long as you are happy and safe'. There was another pause and then he had added, 'I don't mind what you are, as long as you give me a couple of grandchildren at some point or other'.

A few years later, not long after I met John, Dad was killed in a car crash, along with his third wife, who was also my mother's sister (I said it was complex). They were coming back from a night out and their deaths came as a terrible shock. By that time my mother was living in Australia with my older half-brother, Paul. When Mum and Dad had got together it had been a second marriage for both. He'd had a son, Brandon and a daughter, Shae, and she had Paul and then together they'd had me. I didn't know that the other three were only my half-siblings until some rather unkind, or perhaps thoughtless grandparents, pointed out that I wasn't actually their grandchild.

I was heartbroken when Dad died and what he said to me about grandchildren stayed with me through the years. Perhaps because it was something that had clearly meant a lot to him. And perhaps because it was something I wanted too. I loved the idea of having a child. So did John – both of us felt that we would be good fathers. We'd certainly had a dummy run with the dogs, who required more patience and time than most of the children we knew.

As a gay couple we couldn't become parents without intervention from outside. We thought about adoption, but we both felt that we would like a child that was biologically ours. So, although the idea of parenthood was dusted off from time to time, we never got any further with it. Until one night I saw a documentary about surrogacy in India.

John had an early start for work most mornings, so he would often go to bed before me, taking Remus and Gracie with him. One night, channel surfing for something to watch, I came across 'Made in India'. It was about a Western couple who were able to have children with the help of an Indian surrogate and it said that India was a hub for international surrogacies. I was fascinated. This was an ordinary couple and if it had worked for them, why not us? For the first time I had discovered something that seemed to hold the real possibility of providing us with our own children. I went to bed, squeezing into the small space left on my side by the dogs, and lay wide awake with excitement.

Of course, we knew about the existence of surrogacy, given high profile cases like Elton John and David Furness, singer Ricky Martin and actress Sarah Jessica Parker and her husband Matthew Broderick, all of whom had children using surrogates. But until that documentary I had never thought that it might be a route open to us too.

I decided to do some more research before putting the idea to John. I needed to know what would be involved. I knew it would be costly, but by this time John's business was doing well, he had new offices in the city and, despite the recession, plenty of clients.

One evening, a week or so after I saw the documentary and had my parenthood epiphany, I decided to broach the subject with John. I had looked into it enough by then to know that it was potentially viable for us. We talked for a while, drank some white wine, and talked some more. It was all positive, but at that stage very contemplative. He was keen, but more cautious than I was; he had a lot of questions. However, we both realised that, give or take a few reservations and concerns, we wanted the same thing – to become fathers. The logistics might take some time to plan, and our concerns might not all be identical, but the idea had the green light from both of us.

It was probably the most significant conversation we'd ever had in our lives together.

Since it was important to both of us to have a child that was biologically ours, we agreed that we would like two children, one John's one mine. We would hope to have them conceived at around the same time by two surrogates so that they would be born at the same time, perhaps even using the same egg donor. That way the children would be both genetically related and genetically ours.

We set out to discover everything we could about surrogate babies. There were a few countries where the surrogacy business was thriving: Ukraine, India, America and, of course, the UK. There were also different kinds of surrogacy. In the UK there was only what was known as altruistic surrogacy in which the surrogate was not allowed any financial gain, only expenses. The danger with this was that the surrogate mother was more likely to feel she had a claim over the child or children and in several cases the surrogate had refused to hand over the child. The law was on the surrogate's side for the first six weeks, whether or not she was the egg donor. She was the one who had given birth and she could keep the child if she wished to. Even after that, the surrogate could stay involved if she wanted to.

This idea might have been perfect for some couples, but we were both worried about possible problems at a later date. We didn't want a part time 'mummy' calling in every now and then to check on us and we didn't want any confusion for the children. Our children would have two parents – us. Two daddies who had planned to have them and who would love and support them always. Of course, we would explain how they came into the world, but we would be the ones raising them.

Despite this we did look seriously at the altruistic surrogacy option. John felt that it might work for us, and at one point we had a cleaner who we were pretty sure would gladly have offered to be our surrogate. But before we could ask her, we discovered that she had been stealing from us and we had to fire her. After that the altruistic route seemed just too fraught with danger, which meant that we needed to choose the alternative – compensated surrogacy. More expensive but cleaner and simpler. You paid the surrogate a fee and the child would be legally yours. This was not legal in the UK, so we needed to look abroad.

John told me not to rush into anything, but that was like telling a full-speed express train not to rush, I was already so excited I could barely think about anything else. And I was aware that time was not on our side. We were in our forties and getting on, in new dad terms, so we needed to get going.

We decided that if we went to the Ukraine, we might have language problems, so I started looking into surrogacy in America and in India, where English is widely spoken. After a lot of research, we narrowed things down to the Fertility Clinic of California and the Rotunda Clinic in Mumbai.

I started by calling the Californian clinic. As I dialled, I was rigid with nerves – this was going to be the first time I would tell anyone that we were planning to have a baby. What had, until then, been an idea was about to become very real.

'Good morning, Fertility Clinic of California, Tammy speaking, how may I help?'

My heart was pounding as I blurted, 'Hello, I want, no we want a baby, we're going to have a baby, I need information, we're in the UK, can you help us?'

'Please Sir, slow down, you are sounding rather discombobulated.'

Discombobulated! What on earth did that even mean?

I took a few deep breaths and started again. 'Please, can you send us some information? We are a gay couple in the UK considering having a baby (or two) via IVF and surrogacy.'

At this point, I barely understood the meaning of phrases like IVF Cycle and Gestational Surrogacy, although I would later get to know them and their connotations inside out.

Tammy said she would send us the catalogue and the price list and moments later they pinged into my email inbox.

We knew that whatever route we took would be expensive. But the Californian clinic's price list shocked us. It was endless; consultation fees, clinical fees, IVF fees, legal fees, donor fees, surrogate fees, hospital fees... the list went on and on. And every section had perhaps 20 additional sub-categories with even more fees listed. On top of which there were insurance premiums for just about everything.

Reading through it all we could see our nest egg evaporating – and then some. We were looking at $150,000 per pregnancy. It was scary.

India, then.

My next call was to the Rotunda Clinic, where I spoke to Doctor Somya. She sounded very friendly, and she reassured me that the cost of the whole procedure would be in the region of $55,000 per pregnancy. A third of the cost in America. She said they were very supportive of same-sex couples, and she made it all sound very straightforward. The first step was for us to go over to India to make our sperm deposits which would then be frozen. After that they would inform us when suitable surrogates were found. And in the meantime, we would be sent a choice of egg donors. We had Lift off!

Chapter 2

Preparing for Parenthood

We stepped off the plane at Chhatrapati Shivaji Maharaj International Airport into the sultry heat of an Indian night.

After queuing through customs, we got into a taxi and gave the driver the name of our hotel. As we wove our way through the streets, we could see why Mumbai is called the city that never sleeps. It was the middle of the night, but there were people thronging the streets and stalls selling food on every street corner. The noise of the rickshaw horns, voices calling, and music playing was loud even with the taxi windows up. And the scent was almost overpowering; the air was thick with the aromas of spices, people, animals, and traffic fumes. This was India's biggest city, home to over 20 million people – and holder of all our hopes.

We were in a whole new world. I looked at John. Could this be happening – would this extraordinary place give us the children we longed for?

It was late October 2011 and it had been several months since my first conversation with Somya. Since then, we had exchanged numerous emails, outlining all that would be involved and cementing our agreement. Finally, everything was in place, and she told us to arrive at the clinic, where she would be waiting for us.

We'd got our tourist visas within a few days and booked our tickets the moment John could get a few days away from work. Remus and Gracie were safely settled in a boarding kennel, and we were on our way.

The Rotunda Clinic was based in Bandra West, a middle-class suburb, so we'd chosen a hotel nearby. As we only had three days in India, we'd gone for five-star comfort and as we stepped out of our taxi outside the Taj Lands' End Hotel, I was struck by the levels of security on show. There were at least eight guards on the door, every car was checked inside, and underneath and all our things had to go through a security scanner. Not surprising, I guess, since this was only three years after the 2008 terror attacks which took place across the city over four days, killing 164 people and wounding 308. Hotels, cinemas, stations, and other public buildings had been targeted.

Now, clearly, our hotel – and as we later discovered, every other hotel and many public buildings – were not taking any chances.

Our room gave us a panoramic view across the southern Mumbai suburbs, beside the impressive Bandra-Worli sea link which stretched over the water towards the point known as Lands' End and the famous Bandra Fort, a watchtower built by the Portuguese in 1640, when they occupied this part of India.

Beyond it lay the Arabian Sea. All wonderfully romantic, but by then we were so tired that we simply fell into bed, exhausted.

The following day we took a rickshaw to the Rotunda Clinic. The route took us along the Bandstand Promenade which stretches for about a kilometre along the seafront. The Rickshaw driver spoke no English and our Hindi was non-existent, so I tracked the route on my phone and pointed to where we wanted to go. The only problem was, there were three different addresses on my Google map for the clinic. We picked one, hoping it would be right, and the driver dropped us off. But when we got inside, we were told – sorry, wrong place. Apparently, the main clinic was another 15 minutes' walk away. It was a scorching 37 degrees and by this time we were hot and thirsty, but we walked slowly and, after going up and down the street a couple of times peering at the building numbers, we found it. No sign outside and no front door. We found a door at the back and a security guard pointed upwards.

'Which floor?' I asked. He nodded his head from side to side and smiled. We gave up and took the stairs.

The clinic was on the third level and Somya was there to greet us. It was nice to put a face to the name, after all the months of emailing. She was like an Indian version of actress Caroline Quentin; generously proportioned and friendly. She chatted to us for a bit, asking about our trip, and then we left her office and went to pay the fee for this stage of the process, the 'drop off and cryo' which basically meant freezing our sperm.

We sat in the waiting room until called to make our deposits. John went in first and emerged within five minutes holding a plastic beaker which was taken from him by a very short and unsmiling Indian nurse. He winked at me and sat down, after which the nurse indicated that it was my turn and handed me another plastic beaker.

Inside the small room I did a double take. All four walls were covered with posters and cut-outs of what can only be described as 1970's Swedish porn. It was all big boobs and pouting blondes. So much for their gay customers! Come to think of it I'm fairly sure what was on offer wouldn't have appealed much to many of their hetero customers, especially the Indian ones who might be there to begin the process of IVF with their wives.

All I could do was close my eyes, breathe deeply and think of – anything other than what was on the walls. Five minutes later I emerged with my beaker, which I handed to the nurse. Job done.

Somya assured us that we would be informed as soon as two suitable surrogates were found and that was it – we were free to go.

We had two more days in India, and we spent them absorbing the myriad of colours, the scents, intoxicating and otherwise, and the vast panoply of life in Mumbai. We walked along the Bandstand, joining the crowds of lovers and families strolling along, taking the air, and admiring the view. It was one of the city's most popular hangout spots and all of Indian life was there. Small stalls sold peanuts in paper horns or coconut water, beggars held out their hands, joggers passed us, groups were going through yoga routines and women in saris of every hue floated past.

We were very conscious of the dramatic contrast between rich and poor. Next to our luxurious hotel there was a shanty town, its tiny ramshackle shelters and narrow alleyways teeming with people, most of them children, dressed in rags.

It was the same everywhere we went; behind every glamorous building – and there were many of those – there was a desperately poor community struggling to survive. It made us feel uncomfortable, although later during my time in India I became tougher and more immune to the constant pleas for money. Working it out as a Westerner is difficult, but there is no choice other than to toughen up.

Wherever we went the air was filled with a thousand scents; food cooking, bodies, animal dung, stagnant water, rotting vegetables; it was a sensory overload.

After three days we flew home knowing that, if all went well, we might soon be back. The dogs were hysterical with joy to see us and more hyper than ever.

We picked up the threads of our lives, aware that it might be a long wait for our surrogates. We had requested two at once, so that they could have parallel pregnancies. And to complicate things even further, we had stipulated that the surrogates could not be married women. Our research had taught us that our surrogate mothers needed to be single so that our children would be born with British Citizenship by descent. British law dictated that if the surrogate mother was married, her husband would be classed as the child's father. The genetic father to the child was only recognised by the UK authorities if the surrogate mother was single. But while there were quite a few married women coming forward to be surrogates, very few unmarried girls would want to have a stranger's child before marriage. That left young widows – a small pool – and divorcees, an even smaller pool, since in India marriage is generally for life. 'It will not be easy to find what you are looking for,' Somya had said, shaking her head from side to side. We could only wait and hope.

We had hoped to be treated as a couple, but despite the clinic's supposed positive attitude to same-sex partners, we were told that we had to be treated as two single people, quite separate from one another. I felt let-down when Somya explained this, it was clear that in her early conversations with me she'd been telling porkies when she talked about us being treated by the clinic as a couple.

We agreed to let it go – as long as the pregnancies worked out, all would be fine. We just had to keep the end-goal in mind.

As we waited for news, we began making plans. We had decided that, in preparation for starting a family, we needed a country base. Or at least John decided, and I got on board because I remembered how happy I'd been in the Somerset house, The Laurels, where I'd lived as a child. We wanted the best possible childhood memories for our children and the peace and safety of village life seemed preferable to the London rat race.

We still planned to live in London, because of John's job, but the flat, although it had three bedrooms, was fairly small and it had no garden. We pictured the children going to the small school around the corner from the flat and then piling them, with the dogs, into the car to go to the country for weekends and holidays.

At the same time, we decided to get married – or to enter a Civil Partnership, which was the closest thing available (full gay marriage was two years down the line). We had been common-law partners for 17 years by then, but John especially felt that to do things properly we should make our union formal. So, on June 1st, 2012, quietly and with no fuss, we got hitched in the Brydon Room in Chelsea Town Hall. The Brydon room is a large, stylish room with huge windows hung with elegant drapes. There to witness the ceremony were my mother, who came over from Australia for it, plus John's family; his mother Hazel, stepfather Michael, sisters Sara and Judy, their husbands Gerry and Phelim and niece and nephews Georgia, James, and Theo. We also invited around 20 of our good friends. The registrar was a wonderful, rather theatrical gentleman, whom everyone instantly adored.

A couple of weeks later we put down a deposit on our country home. Long River was a beautiful old house in Berkshire which had been converted into several separate homes. John had found it and he insisted I go to see it. We both loved it at first sight, with its impressive architecture and large garden. The home we chose was spread over three storeys, with a majestic flight of stairs and an enormous living room looking out over the terrace to the large garden. We pictured our children running around it at the weekends. This was where we would give them a secure and happy life and wonderful childhood memories.

By this time, we had waited eight months for the clinic in India to find our surrogates, and there was still no news. We had to content ourselves with choosing an egg donor. We had agreed that we would like the same donor for both pregnancies. Donating eggs for a fee was a far easier process that carrying the child, so there were more candidates and the clinic sent us about 20 to choose from. For each we received a photograph, medical statistics, and some information about the woman's education. No names. Many were young women doing it to make extra money for their weddings.

We chose a woman we felt looked wise. She was in her mid-twenties; she'd had no medical problems and she seemed ideal.

Our children would be British citizens and British culturally, but they would be half Indian, so of course we planned to tell them about their Indian heritage too.

In late July, a few weeks after we had married and found Long River, Somya wrote to say that two surrogates, both in their mid-twenties, had been found. Both would have the fertilised eggs introduced at the same time. Eight eggs would be fertilised, four with John's sperm and four with mine and four would then be implanted into each surrogate. This was more than would be allowed under British law and I presume the clinic did this in order to guarantee a better success rate.

We were told that the 'conception' date would be August 7. On day 5 of embryo creation, they would be transferred to each of the surrogates. After that they would let us know if there were signs of pregnancy. We already knew (by this time we knew so much about the whole process that either of us could have won Mastermind) that pregnancy hormones would be detectable after about ten days and the heartbeat at six weeks. So, we wouldn't have long to wait. We held our breath.

There was no email on the day of creation or the day of embryo transfer. And no word for the following few days. I walked the dogs for hours, cooked up a storm, scrubbed the flat – anything to help the time pass.

I was alone at Long River when the phone rang. I snatched it up.

'Greetings Mr Andrew.'

'Hello Doctor Somya, is there any news?'

'There is good news. John's surrogate, Rehanna, has tested positive for the pregnancy hormone and her levels are good. We will monitor her over the next few weeks and keep you posted.'

'That is wonderful news. Thank you, but what about my surrogate?' At this point I could barely breathe.

'Sadly, you were not so lucky on this occasion Mr Andrew, I am sorry. The pregnancy has not continued.' And with that she hung up.

I was stunned. I sat on the sofa, staring at the phone.

John was going to be a father. And I was not.

It felt impossible to take in.

I thought of my father's words, 'as long as you give me a couple of grandchildren'. Now it looked as though I couldn't do that. I felt bereft. For a short while I just sat and wept. Then I pulled myself together and rang John with the news.

He was thrilled, but he realised I was gutted. 'Let's talk when I get home,' he said.

That evening it was tough. I was happy for John and heartbroken for myself. He was euphoric but trying not to show it.

'It will be our child; you know that don't you?' he said.

I did know – we had agreed all along that we wouldn't tell anyone which of us was the biological father of any children we might have. They would be ours, together, no matter what. That thought did comfort me. But it still hurt badly.

I called Somya back a few days later to ask if the egg donor would be willing to try again. She came back to me soon after to say that yes, another attempt would be possible. We would have to wait three months to harvest another lot of eggs and a new surrogate would need to be found, but they still had my semen frozen, and it could be done. That knowledge cheered me.

Eight weeks later she called again.

'Mr John is expecting twins,' she announced. A twin pregnancy would be 35 weeks, she said, so the babies would be born in late March.

Wow. Of course, we'd known that there was a possibility of twins, but the reality was a real wake-up call. Time to get ready for fatherhood.

We kept the good news to family and a few close friends. Both our mothers were delighted. Having got their heads around their sons being gay, they hadn't expected grandchildren from us. When she heard the news that we were, in fact, going to make her a grandmother, John's mother, forthright as ever, said to him, 'Are you sure you and Andi are capable of bringing up kids?' 'Why wouldn't we be?' he told her. 'We're responsible adults, and our children are wanted, unlike so many in this world.'

We spent the next few months driving down at weekends to work on Long River. It needed decorating throughout, and we wanted to do it ourselves, as a labour of love, taking our time and choosing colours as we went along.

As Rehanna's pregnancy progressed, we were sent regular updates and scans, although we weren't told whether we were having boys or girls. In India parents are banned from learning the sex of their babies so that parents can't choose to end pregnancies if they discover they are expecting girls. There is still a huge boy-bias there, since sons will care for parents and daughters will simply cost money to marry off.

We didn't mind at all what sex the babies were. We loved the idea of a couple of girls. Or boys. Or one of each. We spent hours discussing names. We needed to have two boys' names and two girls' names ready, just in case.

For boys we chose Caleb and Oscar. Names that we both liked. For a girl we agreed on Tara. I have always loved the name and it has an Irish connection (think Gone with the Wind) and the same meaning in Hindi and Gaelic - star, so that was a dead cert. The other name we chose was Amritsar. It's the name of the Sikh holy city, where the famous Golden Temple is, but I just loved it as a name. I told John about it and he agreed that it was beautiful.

'What are we going to be called,' I asked. 'Only one of us can be Daddy.'

We mulled it over and eventually agreed that John, as biological father, would be Daddy and I would be Dadda. Later he would tell me that he was jealous because babies say Dadda long before they say Daddy.

That Christmas we invited all our neighbours over for drinks. They were mostly middle-aged, and elderly and one jovial old chap said, 'When we heard a gay couple was buying, we thought, oh good, no children!'

John and I looked at one another.

'Er, well, actually...' we both began.

As we explained that we did in fact plan to have children, and that actually we had a couple on the way, his face fell.

In the midst of mounting joy and excitement, there was more heartbreak for me. The second attempt, in early December, did result in the detection of the pregnancy hormone. But a week later Somya rang to say that the embryo had no heartbeat. To add to my anguish, she asked us for £1000 to carry out an assisted abortion. We were stunned, why would it cost so much? But we were in no position to argue so we transferred the money and I grieved once again. Pregnancies had failed with two different surrogates. Was I the problem? Or was it simply bad luck? There was no way to know. I asked Somya if I could try once more.

'You may not know this Mr Andrew, but the government here in India has banned commercial surrogacy for all single people, including those who are gay. Only heterosexual couples married for a minimum of two years will be allowed to use the services of a surrogate. We are unable to proceed with any further attempts.'

For me it seemed that the journey to having my own biological child was over. John assured me we would try again, but I couldn't see how. I had to find a way to put my sense of loss behind me and concentrate on our future. The twins' birth date was just a few weeks away and we began collecting nursery furniture; cots and prams, blankets and baby grows, double of everything, for the flat and for Long River.

The birth would be on March 25th. 'If you are here on that day, you can meet your babies straight away,' Somya told us. 'Then you can take them home with you.'

We knew it wouldn't be as simple as she made it sound. It might take weeks, possibly even months before we would be allowed to bring the babies to England. They would need British passports before they could get exit visas. Two months earlier the UK Government website advising on international surrogacy had stated that the passport processing time in India was six weeks. A month later that had been altered to eight weeks and that had since changed to three months before settling for four months or more!

We greeted these announcements with increasing dismay. The change in surrogacy laws appeared to be affecting even the British end of things. Unless they were just being bloody minded, which we thought was entirely possible. We were going to have to be prepared for quite a wait.

Our plan was to travel out together and to spend two weeks getting to know the babies. Then John would go home to work, visiting when he could, and I would remain in India with them until we could all travel home together.

'Mr John is the father so he will need a medical visa,' Somya advised. 'You Mr Andrew, not being related to the twins, may apply for a normal tourist visa.' I winced. She certainly had a way with words.

John duly applied for his medical visa, while I got a tourist visa again. Then John was told by the Indian visa processing centre in Middlesex that they were unable to process his visa as the new surrogacy rules did not allow for anyone not heterosexually married for two years to travel on a medical visa in connection with surrogacy. They explained that he would have to resolve this directly with the Indian High Commission in London. This he attempted to do, but at every turn he was stalled. Vague promises were made that the visa would eventually be granted and meanwhile they would not allow John, while the medical visa was pending, to revert to a simple tourist visa. He appeared to be, in effect, banned from going to India for the birth of his children.

With the deadline for the birth drawing close and no sign of the visa, we became increasingly frantic. In an attempt to break the deadlock, John went to the Indian High Commission in

London, where he waited for quite some time in a small, empty room. When eventually someone spoke to him it was to say, 'We have no update on your visa application – it is still pending'.

John, even-tempered and calm in the face of most provocations, was reduced to shouting, 'But my bloody children will be born in seven days, in India and I need to be there.'

The response? 'We will notify you of any outcome in due course.'

When he came home and told me what had happened, we were both torn between dismay and disbelief. We sat slumped and despairing, wondering what on earth to do.

Eventually John, ever practical, took his head out of his hands.

'There's nothing else for it,' he told me. 'You're going to have to go alone.'

Chapter 3

<u>Birth Day</u>

How had this happened?

Here I was, on a flight from Heathrow to Mumbai, on my own. John should have been there with me; we should have been collecting our twins together. But he had been prevented from coming because he was their biological father. While I was free to go and collect them. Despite my frustration I had to give a wry smile at the irony of the whole thing.

Staring into the darkness as we flew east, I felt worried. How was I going to cope with two small babies on my own? Somehow the idea of looking after the babies had seemed so much less daunting when I thought we'd be doing it together. Wishing I'd been to a few early-years parenting classes, I stared gloomily out of the window.

John had hugged me goodbye at Heathrow, both of us close to tears. He was certain that he would be able to come out soon – four weeks at the most, he thought. And in the meantime, he had hastily consulted a lawyer and given me Power of Attorney so that I could make all necessary decisions about the children's welfare in his absence.

Heavy-hearted I thought back to our last trip to Mumbai, seventeen months earlier. We had both been so excited about starting the journey towards parenthood. Now the birth of our children was a day away and we should be travelling together to meet them and begin life as a family. Instead, I had to do it for both of us. It was a difficult situation, and I was just going to have to manage. If I didn't know much about caring for new born babies, well, I would learn fast.

We landed in Mumbai early on the morning of March 25th. I hadn't slept a wink throughout the nine-hour flight. Grabbing my bags, I jumped into a taxi and headed for the Novotel at Juhu Beach, on the west coast of the city.

The birth of the twins, by caesarean section, was due that afternoon and I hoped to be able to see them soon afterwards. I was due to speak to Somya mid-morning, but our relationship had become strained since her misjudged advice that John needed a medical visa. Her recent emails had contained one-sentence replies to our questions. Was she going to cooperate now that I was actually here, and the babies were due?

I wasn't even sure which hospital to go to. I called John and told him I had arrived safely, and he'd said he was sure everything would be fine. But after the call ended, I felt alone and ill-prepared. I sat at the desk in my room, staring out at the street below. It would all work out...wouldn't it?

I called Somya, who told me to go to the Hiranandani Hospital where the twins would be born. At least that was the first step sorted. I showered and changed into fresh clothes and then left the hotel and found a taxi in the rank on the other side of the road.

'Hiranandani Hospital' I said. 'How much?'

The driver nodded his head and said '1000 rupees'. That was around £11, exorbitant for a taxi ride; the hospital had to be some distance away. But I had to get there, so I nodded and got in. We drove along the expressway for what seemed like hours. We left the city behind and kept on going.

I leaned forward. 'Are you sure this is the right way?'

'Oh yes sir, Hiranandani Hospital is in Thane, it is north of Mumbai. We are almost there now.'

Ten minutes later he deposited me outside the hospital. I asked him to wait, since I wasn't sure how long I would be there or how I would find a taxi back.

In the maternity unit I found a nurse and asked her where I could find the surrogate mothers. She led me to the Sister, who spoke some English. 'I am sorry Sir,' she said, 'We have no ward for surrogate mothers here; I believe you want Hiranandani Hospital in Powai'.

I stared at her in disbelief. 'There are two Hiranandani Hospitals?'

'Yes,' she nodded. 'And you are definitely in the wrong one.'

I rushed back outside to find the taxi still waiting. Sliding into the back seat I asked him where the other Hiranandani Hospital was.

'Oh,' he smiled. 'That Hiranandani Hospital is back in Mumbai. Where we came from,' he added helpfully.

Had he not thought to ask me which one I wanted? I didn't even try asking that, I just told him to take me to the other one.

An hour and a half later we arrived outside a large rectangular, white building with a pillared entrance. By this time, I was very hot, cross, and suffering from lack of sleep, plus jetlag as a result of the five and a half hour time difference.

'We are here Sir. That will be 2000 rupees,' the driver said, still smiling.

I paid him and then called Somya to ask her why she hadn't told me there were two hospitals with the same name. The connection was bad, and I couldn't understand what she was saying. Then the line went dead. I stared at my phone – had she just hung up on me? How dare she?

Clearly things were going from bad to worse. I just had to hope all would go well with the birth and the handing over of the twins. Somya I would reckon with later.

At the entrance there was the usual cabal of security guards who frisked me and searched my bag.

Inside I found myself in a large reception area, where I headed for one of two receptionists.

'I am here for the surrogate Rehanna Khan and the expected birth of twins today?'

'You will need to go to the hospital social workers' office, just behind this reception to your right,' she said.

I found the social workers' office, but I could see through the glass window that there was no-one there. I knocked anyway, in case one of them was hiding under a desk. No reply. With no choice but to wait, I crossed to the nearby waiting area, close to a Hindu shrine of the deity Ganesh and took a chair between an elderly man and a pregnant woman.

This wasn't going well. Perhaps the babies were here by now. Would I even get to meet them today? My head buzzed, but I could only wait and see. Surely my day had to get better at some point...

Half an hour later two social workers, a man and a woman, arrived back from their lunch breaks at the same time.

'Hello,' I said, 'I am here for the twin births of surrogate Rehanna Khan.'

'OK Sir, please come and sit down,' one of them said. 'I am Santos, and this is Maria.' He indicated the other social worker, who had come into the office with us.

I fumbled through the sheaf of documents in my bag and passed him the Power of Attorney, the Surrogacy Agreement naming me as John's next of kin and our Civil Partnership Certificate, showing that I was his spouse. This combination of documents should have been enough to verify who I was, my connection to the twins and my right to see them. But Santos was shaking his head.

'Forget about this document,' he said, passing back the Civil Partnership Certificate. 'Indian authorities do not acknowledge this. You will need to go to a notary office and have a statement notarised on stamped paper and signed by the notary, a government-appointed legal practitioner, explaining that you have this Power of Attorney and, as the next of kin, in John's absence, will be acting as Guardian to the babies.'

'But surely the Power of Attorney and the Surrogacy Agreement give me that right, even without the civil partnership,' I protested.

'I am sorry Mr Andrew,' Maria said. 'Here in India, you will need this additional notarised document, tying these two documents together. Then you may see the babies. There are many notaries in the city, just ask and you will be directed to one.'

There was no point in arguing. Promising I would be back, I picked up my papers and my bag and headed back outside, where I jumped into a passing rickshaw.

'Notary office please'.

'Huh? What is this?'

I got out my phone and looked up Notary Office in Powai and an address popped up. I showed it to the driver, and he nodded and set off. Fifteen minutes later we stopped outside a residential address. I knocked on the door.

A young man answered the door. 'Notary Office?' I asked.

'No, sorry,' he said. Then he added, 'There is an area a few kilometres from here where there are several notaries.' He spoke to the driver in Hindi. The driver nodded and beckoned me back into the rickshaw.

We drove for 45 minutes through the bustling, honking Mumbai traffic until we reached one of the poorer districts, where tiny passageways criss-crossed one another and most 'shops' were simply open counters in the doorway of a small house. The driver stopped at the end of one of the passageways and pointed to it. 'Down there,' he said. I thanked him, paid, and asked him to wait for me. He pointed to a teashop across the road. 'You will be some time. I will be there,' he said.

How long was this going to take? I headed down the alleyway, clutching my bag, which contained not only the precious legal documents but my money and passport, tightly under my arm.

There was no sign anywhere saying, 'Notary Office'. Why had I thought there might be? I was rapidly learning to adapt my expectations. I had to ask half a dozen vendors before I found my way to a small staircase leading up to a tiny, very hot waiting room where I sat for the next hour.

Finally, I was ushered into the office, another tiny room where a middle-aged man in a well-pressed, button-down white shirt sat at a desk covered with mountains of files and papers. Beside him a small electric fan whirred half-heartedly on a side table, blowing hot air from one side of the room to the other and making no difference at all to the stifling heat. He smiled and stood up to shake my hand. 'I am sorry to have kept you waiting. I am Mr Chowdhury, the notary. How can I help you?'

I explained the situation to him and dug out the relevant paperwork.

'Ah, Mr Webb, I am sorry you've had to come all this way. This problem can be easily sorted.'

He took a statement from me tying the Power of Attorney and Surrogacy Agreement together and then printed it onto the thin, officially stamped paper used for legal documents. After that there were several official rubber stamps and he signed it. Job done. Thanking him I headed back up the alleyway to where I had left the rickshaw. I found the driver, as promised, in the tea shop and we headed back to the hospital where I rushed to the social workers office.

It was empty.

'They have gone home for the day,' the hospital receptionist told me. 'You will have to come back tomorrow.'

'But they can't have gone. They knew I was coming back. My babies have been born this afternoon and I need to see them. Surely there is some other social worker on duty in the evening?'

She smiled. 'I am sorry, there is no social worker until 9am tomorrow. Come back then.'

I stood looking at the stairs leading up to the wards. Somewhere up there our twins lay, waiting for me. Had the birth gone as planned? Were they alright? It seemed so cruel that I would have to wait another night to find out. But in India, as I was discovering, waiting was a way of life – as much a part of most people's existence as eating and sleeping. To the unavoidable in life, death and taxes, India has added, 'waiting'.

I made my way back to the hotel, sad and frustrated. A phone call to John didn't help. He had gone to the Indian High Commission first thing to tell them his children were being born that day, only to receive a totally disinterested, 'your visa is being processed, we will notify you when it is ready'.

After a cold beer and a meal, I fell into bed completely exhausted. Tomorrow... I thought, as I slipped into a dreamless sleep... tomorrow everything will be different. Tomorrow I will meet our children and start to make plans to take them home.

The following morning, I was back at the hospital by nine. Maria and Santos were in their office, and they seemed delighted to see me, which was encouraging.

'Is everything in order Mr Andrew?' Maria asked.

I got out the notarised statement and gave it to her. She read it and handed it to Santos.

'Perfect,' he beamed. 'You can see your babies today.'

'So, they're well, everything is alright? Can I see them now?'

'They are fine, all is well. But you can't see them yet. Visiting hour begins at 10am. You can see them then and if you would like you will be able to feed them also.'

'Yes, please, I'd like that very much. I'll go and get a coffee and come back at 10. I turned to go and then suddenly remembered something.

'I'm so excited I almost forgot to ask. What sex are the babies?'

Maria smiled. 'You and John have two beautiful baby girls. I hope you like the colour pink!'

'Girls,' I said, 'oh that's perfect. We have two girls.'

I couldn't take it in. At last, after all the stress of the last few weeks, it was beginning to feel real. We were parents.

'Have you chosen names' Maria asked?

'We have. Tara and Amritsar.'

'They are very lovely names. You will have to decide who has which name. See you in half an hour.'

Too excited to sit down, I paced the reception area, clutching a cardboard cup of coffee from the hospital coffee shop. By five to ten I was back at the office.

Maria took me up to the hospital's fourth floor, where she asked me to take a seat while she spoke to the Staff Sister. I could see them nodding and pointing in my direction and then Maria came back and said, 'You will be called shortly. Good luck!' She disappeared back down the stairs and I sat, tense as a racehorse at the starting gate, watching the Sister bustle off through a set of double doors and willing her to hurry up.

At that point, another door opened and a trolley-cot containing a small baby emerged, followed by two men. They were conversing with one another in Hebrew but broke into English as a doctor emerged behind them.

'We are so happy with this moment Doctor Soni,' one of them said.

'A very healthy three and a half kilos,' the doctor replied. 'Congratulations.'

The doctor, who I discovered had also delivered our girls, rushed off and one of the men fumbled in his pocket for a phone and then came over to me.

'Please can you photograph us together,' he asked.

'Of course,' I replied. 'Boy or girl?'

One of the men picked the baby up and showed him to me, grinning from ear to ear. 'Boy,' he said. 'Our first child.'

I took several photos of the two proud dads with their small boy.

'I am Alon, this is Saul, and this is baby Avi,' said the one holding the baby.'

'Nice to meet you, I'm Andi. 'I'm just waiting to meet our two girls,' I told them.

'Congratulations,' they laughed. 'That's wonderful.'

It felt so good to be congratulated as a new dad. All I needed now was to actually see my children.

'Maybe see you again Andi,' Alon called as they disappeared into the lift.

'I hope so,' I called after them.

I hoped I would see them again. It felt so heartening to be among people on the same mission.

Just then the Sister re-emerged through the double doors.

'Mr Webb,' she said. 'You can see the babies now. They are on the second floor, in the Neonatal Intensive Care Unit – the NICU.' I must have looked alarmed because she went on, 'Don't worry, there is nothing wrong with them, they are not premature, it is usual for twins to spend a few days there when they are smaller at birth than single infants. Tell the reception there that you are here to see Rehanna Khan's twins on behalf of the father.'

I bounded down the stairs to the second floor where I went to the reception desk and told the stern-faced receptionist that I was there to see Rehanna Khan's babies.

'So, you are not the babies' father?'

'No,' I said through gritted teeth. 'I am his civil partner. Please call down to Maria the social worker and check if you need to. They have all the paperwork.

'Wait here,' she said.

Half an hour passed before she returned. 'You need to bring the paperwork here to us.'

There was now only 15 minutes of the visiting hour left. Afternoon visiting wasn't until four – almost five hours away. Surely, they weren't going to make me wait until then.

I shot back down to the social workers office. They were out.

An agonising hour later Maria reappeared. I explained the situation and she frowned. 'They shouldn't need to see the paperwork again. But wait a minute, I will get it.'

I headed back up the stairs with the papers and handed them to the receptionist, who was reminding me more and more of Nurse Ratched from One Flew Over the Cuckoo's Nest.

'Wait here,' she said.

She disappeared with the papers. By the time she returned it was past 12.

'Come back at 2pm,' she said. 'You will be permitted to see the babies then.'

Fine. Back down the stairs again – at least I had to be getting fitter, I thought – I went out and found a cafe where I could sit and wait over a lunch of samosas.

At one-thirty I went back to the hospital and took up position beside the NICU reception, where Nurse Ratched pointedly turned her back to me.

Finally, at five past two, a nurse approached me. 'Come this way, please,' she said.

At the door of the NICU I was asked to take off my shoes and to put on a pink hospital gown, a pink hairnet, and a pink mask. I was relieved that I couldn't see myself.

It was hot and I was nervous as I followed the nurse past four Perspex incubator cots to two at the far end of the ward, one on each side. They were labelled Rehanna Baby One and Rehanna Baby Two. In the cots lay two perfect small girls, each one swamped by an outsized nappy. Each had a mop of jet-black hair and eyes tight shut.

'They are very healthy,' the nurse said.

'Can I touch them?'

'Yes, put your hand in through the hole in the side of the cot.'

I slipped my hand into the first cot and held the baby's tiny hand for a minute. Then I did the same with the other. Minute fingers curled around mine. 'Which one is the oldest?'

'This one weighed two point four kilos, she is heaviest, so she is the first one. The other baby was two point three kilos.' The oldest would-be Amritsar. Her sister would be Tara.

I felt such pride and happiness.

'Welcome to the world little ones,' I whispered. 'I am your Dadda.

Chapter 4

Happy Holi

As I walked along Juhu Beach the night was warm and still, the city murmurings suddenly distant and overhead the full moon was crystal clear and luminous. It seemed auspicious, full of the promise of good things to come. Surely, I told myself, all would be well, John would arrive soon, and we would take our girls home together.

I took off my shoes and held them in one hand as I walked on, the sand cool between my toes and the water lapping at the shore beside me. It was good to feel the sea breeze, and to have space to reflect on another unpredictable day in this extraordinary land.

That morning I had planned to set off for the hospital, as usual, to see the girls. I had visited them the previous morning and once again I had only been allowed a brief time with them during which, garbed as always head-to-toe pink, I held each tiny hand for a couple of minutes and gazed at their perfect faces; their minute noses, barely discernible eyebrows, rosebud mouths and delicate caramel cheeks, framed by tufts of jet-black hair. I hadn't been able to send John a photograph yet – no cameras in the ward, nurse Ratched had admonished sternly when she spotted my phone – so all I could do was describe the babies to him.

After a few minutes I was hustled out by the nurses, who told me that the following day I could stay longer and perhaps even feed the babies. But what no-one had mentioned was that the following day was also the spring festival of Holi – when all of India would erupt in a riot of colour, celebration, and excitement – and going anywhere would prove impossible.

When I came down to the hotel reception in the morning I had been greeted by the receptionist with a beaming smile.

'Good morning, Sir, Happy Holi, have a very good day,' he said.

'Thank-you, you have a good day too.'

What had he said? Happy Holi? What was that I wondered. I stepped outside the hotel and looked around for a taxi. Strangely the usual ranks weren't lined up and waiting. Puzzled, I walked down the road towards the beach, hoping to hail one as I went.

Suddenly I felt a slap on the back of my leg, and I looked down to see a splatter of purple liquid dripping down the back of my calf. What on earth? I turned around. Behind me were three young men, armed with water guns and shoulder bags. As they drew level with me one of them reached into his bag and brought out a handful of yellow powder. He lunged towards me and smacked his hand onto the back of my head.

I yelled and put my hand up to my head, where I could feel the powder. The three of them were falling about laughing and reaching into their bags. Out came red, green, and more yellow.

'Happy Holi,' they called, before hurling the powder at me and spraying me with their water guns which, it turned out, contained the purple dye.

They ran off and I stood looking after them, aghast and dripping a rainbow of colours that must have looked ridiculously comical.

I headed back towards the hotel. Whatever this was – some kind of bizarre tourist-mugging ritual? – I'd had enough. I only had a couple of meters to go to the hotel entrance, but my route was barred by another excited group of young men, also carrying bags and water guns, and covered from head to toe in every colour of the rainbow. As they aimed their guns at me – pink and orange this time – I turned and ran towards the beach. But I soon realised there would be no escape. More and more people, all patchworks of colour themselves, were splattering one another and everyone else within reach.

On the beach music was playing, paint-spattered people were dancing, and the colour-spraying was in full-flow. Intoxicated by the joy and craziness of it all, everyone was singing and shouting. Even the sea, normally a polluted, dull grey at Juhu, was a riot of colour.

I wondered whether to join in the dancing, but being a tourist, I was a key target. As more and more paint and dye came my way I turned and ran for the hotel.

I had left the lobby half an hour earlier, clean, and freshly dressed. I arrived back, gasping for breath as I hurled myself through the revolving door, looking like a crazed hippy living out his psychedelic fantasies. I dropped to my knees and placed the palms of my hands onto the floor. My friend at reception smiled politely.

'I see you have been joining in the Holi celebrations Sir.'

Diplomatically put.

'Er, yes, well, something like that.'

I headed for my room and a very long shower. After which, unable to leave the hotel without risking another rainbow dousing, I settled myself in the bar.

Holi, I discovered, chatting to a friendly member of staff, is the Hindu festival that marks the arrival of spring. Known as the Festival of Colour (I think I got that part) it is a celebration of fertility and love as well as the triumph of good versus evil.

How could I object to a festival that was about such optimism and joy? Even if it did prevent me from seeing my new daughters for a day. I just had to hole up and wait it out. It wasn't until the evening that things calmed down and I was able to venture down to the beach to walk under the glorious full moon as I described the day's events to John.

The following morning everything was back to normal. Taxis lined up across the road and only the odd splash of colour on the road remained to mark the events of the day before.

I reached the hospital and headed for NICU reception, where the duty nurse confirmed that I could feed the babies.

Wonderful news, but I was a bit nervous. What did feeding the babies entail, exactly? I wasn't completely sure.

Gowned up I was shown into the feeding room, where there were a lot of soft furnishings and some rather grubby chairs. The room was very hot and didn't smell all that good. I took a seat between two women, both happily feeding babies and a moment later I was handed one of the girls and a bottle.

I had no idea what to do. I knew the contents of the bottle had to be emptied into the baby, but how?

Looking at the others in the room, I did my best to follow what they were doing. I tentatively nudged the baby's small mouth with the teat of the bottle. She opened her lips and I put the tip of the teat against them and then waited. Nothing happened. Why wasn't she drinking the milk?

I looked around for help, but the maternity nurses across the room were smirking. They clearly saw me as a source of entertainment. I guessed that not many new fathers spent time in this room. The nurses clearly thought that feeding was women's business, and I had no place being there.

I tried again. I was growing more and more tense and the baby – I was so nervous that I wasn't sure whether it was Tara or

Amritsar at that stage – was picking up on that. I nudged the teat into her mouth. She spat it back out again. We'd reached stalemate.

There had to be a knack to this, but they weren't about to show me what it was. I was told to, 'just give the baby the bottle' and that was it.

Relegated to the failure ranks, I handed over both baby and bottle to a nurse and fled, under the scornful eyes of the assembled mothers and nurses.

Standing outside I felt indignant. I wasn't going to be beaten by this. How hard could feeding a baby be? I just needed to get the hang of it. I took a break, cooled down and then went back and asked to feed the other baby, who turned out to be Tara. They brought her and I tried again. I watched a mother across the room. Her baby was sucking noisily at the teat. I pushed the teat more firmly into Tara's mouth, and voila, she sucked. Only for a minute, but she did take some milk, before appearing to lose interest and go to sleep.

I handed her back and left. I would crack the feeding thing – I had to, I reminded myself. Soon the babies would be discharged, after which I would have sole responsibility for making sure they didn't starve.

Galvanised by this prospect I went to look for Doctor Anita Soni, the paediatrician who had delivered the girls. I'd already spoken to her a couple of times, and I liked her, she was a rather eccentric, larger than life character who was always laughing and waving her arms around dramatically.

I found her just coming through the ward doors.

'Doctor, when will the babies be able to leave the hospital?'

'Another week or so,' she said. 'They are doing well.'

She hesitated and then placed a hand on my arm and looked into my eyes.

'I just heard you are here all alone. This will be difficult with two new born babies. I think you must consider the assistance of a nanny while you are here in Bombay.'

I was startled. I hadn't thought about a nanny. But she had a point. I'd be on my own with two babies. And we were in a foreign country. There would be no Tesco or Waitrose deliveries in Mumbai. I didn't even know where the local food store was. And what about baby formula and sterilised water and nappies and – what did babies in India even wear?

I needed to get focussed.

'Would the hospital be able to recommend a nanny agency?' I asked her.

'No, I'm afraid not. I advise you to ask at the hotel you are staying in. If it is one of the hotels recommended by the hospital, they are sure to be able to suggest some options.'

'Thank you for the advice.'

She smiled and hurried off and I turned towards the stairs. I had a week's grace and an awful lot to do.

That afternoon I came back at feeding time, prepared to give it another try, only to be told that the nurses had just fed the babies. 'I'm sorry,' an unapologetic nurse told me. 'The babies were very hungry; they could not wait.'

I settled for half an hour watching them sleep and then told the nurse I would be back in the morning at feeding time.

As I left, I ran into Alon and Saul with baby Avi and they invited me for a coffee. We found a coffee shop nearby with a shady back yard and settled down for a chat. It was the first chance I'd had to talk to others in the same situation. They told me they hoped to be back in Israel within four weeks.

'What? Four weeks!'

'It is normally four weeks for us in Israel,' Alon repeated. How long do you expect to have to wait?'

I was stunned to hear it was so easy for Israeli parents. I gave them a rueful grin. 'To be honest I don't know. The time on the government website advising on international surrogacy said six weeks when we first began. Then it was eight weeks and now it's saying four months.

Saul winced. 'Oh, that's tough. Imagine if you have to stay here for four months. And you are on your own.'

'I won't be for long,' I said, sounding more confident than I felt. 'John will be here soon, and hopefully we can get the passports for the girls in less than the stated time.'

'Really hope so,' they nodded sympathetically.

Alon looked thoughtful. 'You know, we met another couple from the UK yesterday on the ward, they also had a twin birth, the day before your daughters, I think. Maybe you should have a talk with them as they will be probably in the same situation, yes?'

'Absolutely.' I was very keen indeed to meet another British couple who would be fighting the same battle.

After Alon and Saul said goodbye and headed off to their hotel, I went back to Juhu beach and phoned John.

'Find the other Brits,' he said. 'That could be so useful and give you some company too.'

The following morning, after another determined – and ultimately doomed – attempt at feeding the girls, I waited in the reception area to see if I could spot the British couple. No sign of them, but ten minutes later I got talking to a couple from Denmark, Tobin, and Thomas. Their daughter had been born a few days earlier and they were waiting for her to be discharged.

'We're staying at the Marriot Hotel,' Tobin said. 'The Lakeside Chalet one. We know the couple you mean; they're staying there as well. They have a boy and a girl, and I think they're taking them home from the hospital today. Why don't you nip down to the main reception and see if they're there?'

I thanked him and shot down the stairs to reception. At the counter stood a couple, each of them holding a car seat with baby in situ. I went over to them.

'Are you guys from the UK?'

They both turned to me.

'Yes,' they exclaimed. 'You too?'

'Yes. My girls are upstairs, they won't be discharged for a few days. But I heard about you guys and wanted to say hello. Seems we might be here for a while so it would be nice to know some fellow Brits. I'm Andi, by the way.'

'Kayla,' the woman, blonde, attractive, and friendly, held out her hand.

'And I'm Jamie.' The man was a little older, his grey hair tinged with pond green.

'See you've been enjoying Holi,' I grinned.

'Yes,' he said ruefully, raking his fingers through his hair. 'Damn stuff won't come out. Think I might have permanently green hair now.'

'Suits you darling,' Kayla laughed. 'It'll soon be all the rage.'

'These two are Millie and Max, by the way,' Jamie said, indicating the babies sitting serenely in their car seats like two mini-Buddhas.

'Hello guys,' I waved down at them.

'We're staying in the Lakeside Chalet hotel,' Kayla said. 'Where are you?'

Over on Juhu Beach, but I think perhaps I ought to move to your hotel,' I said. 'Everyone seems to be there.'

'Oh! do come,' Kayla said. 'Jamie will have to go home soon, and I could do with some company. And the Lakeside gives a 15 percent discount to surrogate families.'

'Why don't you come over this evening and join us for a beer,' Jamie said. 'We've got a nanny booked so we'll have a babysitter, and we can head to the bar for an hour or two.'

'That sounds great,' I said.

That afternoon I went for a stroll around Mumbai. I was going to be there for a while, so I wanted to get a sense of the place. I hadn't had a lot of time for sightseeing, which was a shame since I was in such a vibrant and exotic city. As I walked through a street market selling every kind of spice and vegetable under the sun, I thought about Kayla and Jamie. I felt hugely relieved to have met them, they were friendly and would be good company and they were also relying on the British government to give their children passports and allow them to come home with their parents. It didn't seem so much to ask, but it could apparently take months to achieve.

I walked into the bar of the Lakeside that evening and saw Kayla chatting to another couple. I went over.

'Andi, hi,' she smiled. 'This is Sophie and Pete. He's just been posted here and they're waiting to find a house to rent. Jamie's at the bar, I'll go and tell him to get you a drink.'

As I watched her head over to Jamie she stopped twice to speak to other people on the way.

Clearly Kayla, outgoing, sociable, and high-energy, knew everyone in the hotel. Jamie was quieter, more reserved, but equally warm.

'I'm glad you're going to be about,' he confided. 'Kayla will need a friend when I go. It won't be easy managing here on her own.'

'I'll be happy to help her,' I said. 'But to be honest I think I'll probably need her more than she needs me.'

'Either way it's a good deal,' he laughed. 'You'd better move over here tomorrow.'

I agreed. The next day I checked out of my hotel and moved into a room at the Lakeside Apartments, as it was known by its residents. It had five floors, each with some 20 one-bedroom suits, a couple of two and even three bed apartments and a laundry.

It overlooked the Powai Lake, right in the middle of Mumbai. The lake was created when the British dammed a tributary of the Mithi River in the 1890s to create an extra source of drinking water for the city. Sadly, the water was now too polluted to drink, but I was glad of the lake, every now and then it sent a cool breeze wafting through my windows.

Over the next few days, in between hospital visits and feeding sessions, I went out and bought the baby things I would need; formula, nappies, vests, and baby grows, baby shampoo and lotion, bouncy chairs, and a cot. In fact, the list, compiled under Kayla's direction, was so extensive that I was amazed. How could two very tiny people need so much stuff?

'You'll be surprised what they get through,' Kayla said darkly, when I questioned the need for quite so much infant clothing.'

'I haven't stopped being surprised since I got here,' I replied.

By the time the girls were ten days old I was longing to take them back to the hotel with me. Visiting them in hospital for half an hour at a time, with nurses constantly hovering about, was frustrating. I want to get to know them properly and that would only happen when I had them in my care. So, I was pleased when Doctor Soni told me the girls were doing well and could go home the following day.

I arrived at the hospital bright and early the following morning with two car seats.

Before we could leave there were documents to be sorted and, inevitably, bills to be paid. I also needed the girls' state-registered birth certificates. I spent at least two hours going between the registrar's office in the hospital, the accounts office, and the ward, where I needed Dr Soni's signature for a form before the certificates could be issued. She couldn't be found, and I was beginning to think that I wouldn't be taking the girls home that day after all, when the registrar's office said they would get the signature and then send an 'agent' to the hotel with the birth certificates, for a fee of 300 US dollars. Reluctantly,

I agreed, knowing that I could spend many more hours in the hospital and still not have the certificates.

This was the first time an agent was mentioned to me, but certainly not the last. As I was to discover in the coming weeks and months, there was an 'agent', for which read middleman (or woman) for just about every step of every transaction, all eager for their 'fee' for something that should have been totally straightforward.

Once this arrangement had been put in place, I paid the fees for the babies' care and for Rehanna's caesarean and her hospital stay. It was £1200 for each baby and £600 for the caesarean a total bill of £3000. All these 'extras' had not been mentioned by Somya when she outlined what it would cost us. I winced at the thought of telling John just how fast the bills were piling up, but there was no choice.

Finally, I was done, and the babies were brought out by two nurses and tucked gently into the car seats.

'You need two people, one to carry each baby' Nurse Ratched said stiffly. 'We insist on this.'

'Well, I have only me, so I'll just have to take one in each hand,' I replied.

She huffed and puffed, but in the end, since a second person was not about to materialise, they let me go. I said goodbye to the staff and thanked them. Five minutes later I stepped outside into the heat of the Indian morning, one car seat gripped firmly in each hand. All Change ahead...

Chapter 5

<u>Hands-on Dad</u>

I manoeuvred my two car seats into the lift at the Lakeside and breathed a sigh of relief. Almost there and so far, both babies were still sleeping. Maybe this parenting thing wasn't going to be so hard after all.

'Oh, my goodness they are gorgeous.'

I hadn't even noticed her; I was so wrapped up in checking on the girls. Standing next to me, a huge smile on her face, was a tall, blonde woman. She was stunning.

'I'm Rene,' she said.

'Nice to meet you. I'm Andi and this is Tara and Amritsar.'

'Oh, such lovely babies. You must be very proud. They're beautiful. 'She bent down to stroke the soft hair on each small head. 'Are they yours?'

'Yes, mine and my partner's. We're from the UK. I'll be staying in India with them until he can come over and we can take them home. Not sure how long that will be.'

'I'll be here for a while too.'

'Are you on holiday?' I asked.

Rene smiled. 'Not exactly. I come from South Africa and I'm with a group here for work.'

'Oh right, well I hope you enjoy your stay.'

As I heaved first one and then the other car seat out of the lift on our floor, Rene held the doors open for me.

'Bye Rene, thanks.'

'See you later Andi,' she called as the doors slid shut.

She seemed nice. I wondered what kind of job she was in India to do. It looked as though there were going to be plenty of new friends around and that would be great, as so far, I'd felt I was on my own.

First things first, though, right now I had two 10-day old baby girls to care for. And they were just starting to wake up and make the kind of whimpers and mewly noises that I was fairly sure meant, 'please feed me.'

I still dreaded feeding time. It never seemed easy or straightforward getting each of the girls to engage and take the teats. And now there was just me to manage the two of them, a lot of my time was going to be spent coaxing them to take their bottles.

That afternoon they settled into their new crib surprisingly fast. I'd put it in the corner of the small living room, and I put a rolled-up towel between them. They were so tiny that there was plenty of room for both. As they slept, I slipped into the adjoining bedroom and called John to report our successful transition from hospital to hotel. At last, I could send him photos of his new daughters, and I did, by the dozen. He was enchanted with them, and desperate to be able to hold them in his arms.

Waiting was awful, for both of us. John was still trying for his medical visa and still being told that it was 'being processed.' It seemed incredibly heartless. We could only hope that it would be granted soon, and meanwhile all I could do was send him photos and descriptions of his children.

'I'm going to take their photo in and show them in the visa office,' he said. 'Maybe that will guilt them into giving me the visa'.

I think we both knew it probably wouldn't, given the stony reception he'd had so far. But we needed to clutch at every straw, no matter how unlikely.'

Tara and Amritsar slept peacefully all afternoon. They even slept uninterrupted as I transferred them back into their car seats and took them downstairs and out to the hotel pool, so that I could have a cigarette and a breath of fresh air.

Back in our room Kayla tapped on the door.

'Can I see them?' she whispered.

'Yes, of course, come in. Just don't wake them up.'

She tip-toed in and stood over the crib.

'They're beautiful Andi.' She paused. 'You do know that sleeping all day means they'll probably be awake half the night, don't you?'

'Um, no, I didn't realise that. Don't babies this young sleep all the time?'

'No,' she laughed. 'They sleep about two-thirds of the time. So, if they've been sleeping all day, be prepared.'

She slipped out, suggesting we meet by the pool with all four babies the next day. Jamie had just gone back to England, so she was up for some company. I closed the door behind her and gazed at my sleeping girls. I was a bit worried now, but what could I do? Wake them up so that they'd sleep later?

I decided not to do that. They looked so peaceful. I tried to get some rest myself, but as it was early evening, sleep was impossible. I sent for some supper and settled down with a book. It would be fine, I told myself. After all, how bad could the night be?

If only I had known.

The following morning Kayla called. 'How are things?' she said, sounding ridiculously bright and chirpy.

'Awful,' I croaked. 'I don't think I've slept all night. The minute I put one down, the other would wake. It seemed to be a non-stop round of feeding and walking them up and down and humming to them and nothing seemed to work...'

'Hmmm.' I could almost hear Kayla resist the urge to say, 'Told you so.'

'You need a night nanny,' she said. 'I have Riah and she's wonderful. She manages the babies while I get some sleep.'

It sounded so appealing. But surely things wouldn't be this tough for long? 'Thanks, I'll think about it,' I said.

'OK, see you down by the pool in an hour.'

It had been a long, lonely night. I'd had no idea looking after people so small could be quite so time-consuming and arduous. Or that a baby's cry could by-pass all logic and cut straight to your heart. I prided myself on being a strategic, analytical thinker, but that went out of the window when the girls cried. I couldn't bear the idea of leaving either of them in distress, so at the first small cry I would leap up, picked up whichever baby was crying, and set about soothing and comforting.

Cheered by Kayla's call I had a shower and got the girls fed and changed – I was getting good at the nappies but getting their arms and legs in and out of vests was definitely a challenge – and with a car seat in each hand and a beach bag over my shoulder – headed downstairs.

By the pool I parked the car seats, placed a towel over the top of each one for shade, and settled down for some breakfast, a cigarette, and a nap. I spotted Rene on the other side of the pool, laughing with a group of fellow Amazonian beauties. She waved and I waved back.

In the afternoon I tried to keep the girls awake for a bit. But just as nothing the night before had settled them, now nothing would wake them. The moment they were fed they nodded off again, the heat of the day proving utterly soporific. I tried to take advantage, snoozing while they slept. But any kind of proper sleep was impossible.

That night I put the girls to bed and told them firmly that I needed some sleep and they had better start learning that night was sleep time and day was the time to be awake. Two pairs of eyes looked solemnly up at me and, minutes later, closed.

Success, I told myself. They're off. I think they got the message.

What foolish optimism. An hour later both babies were awake and bawling. What to do when two are crying at once? I ended up pacing the room with one in each arm. After an hour of walking, rocking, singing and (in desperation) describing the view to them, they finally appeared to be asleep. How to put one down without waking the other? Pretty much impossible, as I discovered. Each time I slid one baby into the crib, the other woke and the whole cycle started again.

The night wore on and on...and on. By morning I had decided to go the night nanny route. It was that or insanity via lack of sleep.

As soon as the hour was decent, I called Kayla. She told me she'd heard that a nanny called Bharti was available; she had been working for two Israeli men who had just left. Calls were hastily made, arrangements put in place and Bharti started work that evening, arriving promptly at eight.

Small, round faced, middle-aged and exuding competence, I liked her from the moment we met. She promptly swaddled both girls in brightly coloured cotton wraps and laid them down to sleep like two miniature mummies. Bharti stayed with them in the living room while I, torn between guilt and deep relief, slipped away to the bedroom.

After two nights without sleep I sank into a deep, grateful slumber and knew nothing for the next ten hours, until Bharti gently shook me awake to tell me it was seven in the morning. Both babies, freshly changed and fed, were gurgling happily.

At that point I personally elevated Bharti into sainthood. She stayed with them until eight, giving me time to go and get some breakfast before beginning the day shift.

From then on things went smoothly, with me on days and Bharti on nights. I learned how to get the girls into a routine with changing, feeding and sleeping. We spent several hours a day by the pool, where I chatted to Kayla and we sneaked a cigarette or two, as all four babies slept in their car seats under artfully draped towels.

Bharti, who arrived every night at eight, always dressed in bright, jewel-coloured saris, not only took care of the nights, sleeping on the floor beside the babies' crib, she also taught me the knack of bottle-feeding. How to keep the baby upright, keep the milk in the teat so that air didn't get in and how to remind the baby to feed by tapping the bottle, or turning the teat gently round in her mouth. It all seemed so simple, yet these little techniques made a huge difference to feeds. She also taught me how to wind the babies fully after feeds, rubbing their backs while sitting them on my lap or holding them over my shoulder. I was soon a dab hand at all of it.

Tara and Amritsar looked very alike; they were more like identical twins than fraternal, but from the start I always knew who who was. Not only because of small physical differences, like Amritsar's large almond-shaped eyes, which had been blue at birth, until they turned brown, but because their different personalities were emerging. Tara, always noisier and more excitable, was a bit of a Dadda's girl, always preferring to be on my lap rather than Bharti's, while Amritsar was quieter and more docile. I sent John photos every day, so that he could share the small changes in each of the girls that happened almost imperceptibly as they thrived and grew.

With Bharti on duty, I was able to go down to the bar in the evenings. After full immersion in the world of babies it was good to spend time with other adults and to meet new people. Kayla had introduced me to a few people by the pool, but it was the evenings when the place came to life, as children were settled, and adults came out to play.

The Lakeside was full of ever so slightly eccentric characters. In fact, it sometimes reminded me of the cast of an Agatha Christie novel. There were a number of couples, both hetero and gay, there to collect surrogate babies. But there were plenty of others, there in transit for one reason or another.

The Indian carrier Jet Airways used the Lakeside as a base for many of their pilots. Kayla was very friendly with Caroline, an Irish pilot with a crazy sense of humour. I also met Desi, a Bulgarian who, with her pilot husband, was relocating and waiting for a more permanent address. Desi was friends with Sandra and both of them were a lot of fun.

I actually met Sandra for the first time behind the bike sheds, so to speak, both of us sneaking away for a quick smoke. After that she and I shared the occasional naughty cigarette. Sandra was married to Jaques, a French national who was a chemical company manager; they were resettling in Mumbai after a few years in Rio. She was a big personality and wickedly funny, I enjoyed her painfully accurate observations of all the other guests, and we became good friends.

The very first time I left the girls it was with Sandra. I needed to go grocery shopping and Sandra offered to look after them while I nipped to the shops.

Grateful for her help, I settled them both into one car seat and left them sleeping beside Sandra in the corner of the Crimson restaurant, the focal point where we'd all gather to eat and chat. Sandra, lying back, book one hand and the other giving the car seat an occasional rock, waved me off.

I left the compound, through the security gates and walked down the driveway to the main road to hail a rickshaw. I was in the back of the rickshaw, halfway around the lake on my way to Heiko, the supermarket in Powai, when I started to worry. I had only known Sandra for a week, why had I not asked Kayla? Just how well did I know Sandra and Jaques, I wondered. As we sped towards the supermarket, I worked myself into a frenzy, visualising my new friend and her husband checking out in a hurry, bundling the girls into the back of the company car and heading into the darkest depths of India.

Fellow parents might recognise my wild fantasies for the separation anxiety I was feeling at leaving my two new born babies, as I screamed at the rickshaw driver to turn around and go back to the Lakeside.

Fifteen minutes later I arrived back, half-crazed by imagined disasters, and hurled myself through the doors...to find Sandra as I had left her, enjoying her book, and gently rocking the car seat where the babies were fast asleep.

She looked up; no doubt started by my feverish appearance.

'That was quick.'

What could I say?

'I forgot my wallet,' I muttered, slumping onto a seat beside her. 'I'll try again tomorrow.'

Sandra and I went on to become good friends. Eventually she moved out of the hotel and into a glamorous apartment and I missed her. We stayed in touch and a year later we met in London, where she dragged me into a sex aids shop in Kensington High Street, insisting she was buying a gift for a friend.

Then there was Catherine, a solicitor, Ivanna who was in human resources, Josh and Todd, American riggers on contract to India Oil and famously fond of a drink or two. As was John, who was there with his wife Maria and their son Gordon, who John informed us had been named after a certain green bottle of gin. Gordon, a teenager who was used to following his parents about as they lived their expat lifestyle, took this in his stride and informed me that he was off to China soon to go to 'Kung Fu school'. Right.

For several evenings a chap known only as Fred entertained us with his guitar in the hotel restaurant. He managed to get just about everyone singing Beatles songs. He even got me going on an Elvis number – and I don't do a lot of singing.   Rene and her group were there, sounding like a heavenly choir as they all joined in. There was a lot of laughter and warmth between the guests; in some ways it felt as though we were one big, hugely dysfunctional family.

The following day by the pool Kayla nudged me when Rene and her group settled onto some loungers not far away.

I've worked out what they do,' she hissed.

'Really?' I was curious. I had tried and failed to work out what 20 or so stunning South African women were doing in Mumbai.

'They're egg donors,' Kayla said triumphantly.

'What!' I was incredulous. 'How do you know?'

'Well,' Kayla glanced around. 'You see that woman over there...Lauren. She's their mother hen, she shepherds them around and organises things for them. Her friend is Sophie who works with Doran.' I had already met Doran, an Israeli working for a surrogate agency called Tammuz Fertility. He was facilitating surrogate babies for a number of Israeli couples.

'I think Sophie runs the donor side of things,' Kayla went on. 'I'm pretty sure that all those girls are donating eggs for Israeli couples.'

I was amazed. 'Blimey, you've been keeping a close eye on things! I'm impressed by your investigative skills.'

Kayla laughed. 'I just keep my eyes open Andi, it's not that hard to work out.'

By this time my brain was buzzing. Rene, I realised, might just be the answer to my dreams. I still longed to be the biological father of a child. Perhaps, with Rene or one of the others from her agency as donor, it might be possible. Not here in India, since that was illegal now, but somewhere where surrogacy for gay parents was still allowed. I filed the idea away in the back of my mind to investigate later.

The next time Rene and I stopped to chat I asked her for the agency's details. I had liked Rene from the moment we met in the lift, and I had a good feeling about her and the part she might play in giving us another child. I talked to John about it, and he agreed that I should try again, but the question was, where? Researching potential surrogacy destinations, Thailand seemed like a good option. I could travel there from India for a brief visit to make the deposit. Maybe, just maybe, I would still be able to father a child.

With this in the back of my mind it was time to focus on the immediate issues — like how long our passport application for the girls would actually take.

Kayla and I looked on enviously as people of other nationalities got their passports and exit visas for their children and went home. Top marks went to the USA. Their embassy sorted DNA tests soon after the birth and then processed the babies' passports within two weeks. Job done and the Yanks could hop on a plane home. The Israelis were a close second, coming in at four weeks (later we heard this was down to two weeks). Canada and Australia were also around four weeks, and the Scandinavian countries took six weeks. How could it be that the UK nationals had to wait several months? Ridiculous and shameful. But Kayla and I could rant and rave all we liked; nothing was budging.

Doran sympathised with us, and told us that Israel welcomed all new citizens, surrogate babies included, and so had a very positive and helpful attitude. It was good to know that the UK's obstinate and somewhat disapproving attitude was not universally shared – in fact it made the UK seem backward and perhaps even prejudiced.

'Where are you planning to spend the next few months, while we wait for the passports,' Kayla asked me as we lay by the pool one afternoon.

I groaned. 'I'm not sure. I was hoping for a miracle that would speed things up, I guess.'

'Not likely to happen,' she said, sipping an iced water. 'And this place is too expensive. I've been thinking about going down to Goa to wait it out. It's much cheaper, and it's quiet at this time of year, while it's out of season. Why don't you come too?'

It sounded like a good idea. The Lakeside was costing an arm and a leg, so we couldn't stay there much longer. That afternoon I started researching apartments in Goa on my laptop. Kayla was right, they were much cheaper, and I liked the look of the area.

I lived in hope that John would suddenly appear. I missed him and I felt desperately sad that he was missing the girls' early days. It seemed so heartless. Clearly the change of legislation in India, outlawing surrogate births for gay couples and for those heterosexual couples not married for two years (Kayla and Jamie fell foul of this, as they weren't married) had caused the entire system to jam. It seemed cruel, as our babies were already well underway when the law changed.

Before we moved to Goa, I needed to send John all the necessary documents for their British passport applications, most of which had to be supplied by the fertility clinic. Leaving the girls with Bharti, who agreed to stay on one morning, I got a taxi over to the Rotunda Clinic. Somya came out of her office to greet me, smiling broadly. I showed her pictures of the babies and told her I needed the girls' prenatal scans, Rehanna, the surrogate's identity card and her divorce papers, which had to be originals.

Somya waved her arms and assured me that she would get all these documents together and send them over to me.

'There is no hurry,' she insisted. 'Besides, the notarised document can only be signed six weeks after the birth.'

This was true. We also needed a signed and notarised document stating that Rehanna did not want to be a mother to the surrogate children. This wasn't just for the babies' passports though, it was also for a Parental Order, which John and I would need to apply for in the UK, once we were all home. It had to be signed by Rehanna after a six-week cooling off period in which she was, legally, entitled to change her mind.

'You can send me the notarised document later,' I told Somya. 'But I need the rest as soon as possible. We're going to Goa in three days' time, and I need everything before we go.'

Somya insisted that her admin people were dealing with it all and would send it to me, but I didn't trust her. I said I would be back in two days and asked her please to have everything ready.

It was Sandra who borrowed her husband's official car and drove me back to the Rotunda Clinic to collect my documents.

Needless to say, the documents were not ready. Without them the passport applications couldn't even be started, so Somya's nonchalant attitude was infuriating. I couldn't afford to alienate her though, so I remained patient and polite, while insisting she express them to me in Goa as soon as possible. She promised that she would, and I could only hope that she understood how important they were.

I had found a small apartment in Goa and persuaded the indispensable Bharti to come with me. She was even bringing her friend, Geeta, who would share nanny duties with her. With the cost of renting and living in Goa so much lower, we could afford the extra help.

Two days later, bags packed and entourage in tow, I said goodbye to my Lakeside friends and checked out.

'See you down there in a couple of weeks,' Kayla said, kissing us all.

As the doors closed behind us and we climbed into our taxi I tucked one car seat under each arm.

'Come on girls, 'I said. 'We're off to the seaside.'

Chapter 6

<u>Goa</u>

Half an hour later we were deposited at the airport, this time outside the terminal for domestic flights. With Bharti and Geeta each holding one of the girls I followed, dragging three or four bags behind me while scanning the terminal for our check-in desk.

A couple of minutes later a short, rotund man came rushing up to us and shook my hand vigorously.

'I am Sanjay, Bharti's husband,' he said, shaking his head from side to side and up and down in the by now familiar Indian head wobble that I was beginning to understand had many meanings and could be interpreted according to the situation. I took it that his beaming smile indicated it was a gesture of goodwill and benevolence.

'Welcome to our airport Mr Andi. I am working in the international side of the airport with the immigration office, and I am very happy that my wife is going with you. I will come to visit you with my son in a few weeks' time.'

'Oh, right, very nice to meet you Sanjay,' I said. 'We're just looking for our flight.'

'Allow me to show you the way, Mr Andi, and let me help you with your bags. You will find Goa exceedingly pleasant.'

Minutes later, thanks to Sanjay, who waved us off with many wishes for a happy trip, the five of us were checked in and waiting at the departure gate.

Our flight to Goa was only an hour and twenty minutes, and the girls behaved perfectly throughout. Once we were out of the airport the other end, bags once again in tow, we all piled into a taxi and headed for the apartment I had rented, which was in Panaji, a small and very picturesque city and Goa's state capital.

About six hundred miles south of Mumbai, Goa is the holiday state of India, thanks to its many stunning sandy beaches. It was, for many years, a Portuguese colony, and the Portuguese influence had blended with the Indian in the architecture, the food, and the local culture, giving the area its own unique style.

For a long time seen as a party-hangout and hippy paradise, during the peak tourist season from October to February Goa heaves with people hanging out on the beaches, eating the local seafood, and practicing yoga, chanting, or just soaking up the new-age vibe.

From March to June though, it's less popular. It gets hotter and more humid in the build-up to the monsoon, which hits around mid-June. And this is also when the prices drop, so for our purposes it was ideal.

The apartment I had found was small but clean and comfortable and the landlord agreed to let it to me on a weekly basis, as I wasn't sure how long we would need to stay. Within a couple of months, I fervently hoped, the girls' passports would be through, and we could go back to Mumbai and head home.

There were two bedrooms and the two nannies shared one of them with the babies, while I had the other. All four of them slept in a double bed, Bharti and Geeta on the outside with the babies between them in the middle, lying on a towel and swaddled in colourful strips of old saris that Bharti tore up.

Geeta, it turned out, was the mother of Bharti's son's wife and it was most definitely Bharti who was in charge. Geeta, who was of humble origins and illiterate, lived with Bharti's family in Mumbai, dependent on them for food and bed, so she was obliged to toe the line Bharti laid down. Wages had to be handed to Bharti, who would then give Geeta her share, which turned out to be 1000 rupees from the 5000 rupees a day that I paid them.

The two nannies had childcare organised between them and I found myself rather on the outside – they were with the girls 24 hours a day and I felt virtually redundant to requirements. Grateful as I was for Bharti and Geeta's help, this was slightly disconcerting!

I began looking for ways to spend time with the girls without disrupting the nannies' routine.

The high point for me was Bharti and Geeta's shopping trip. Every two days I would give Bharti 2000 rupees and off they would go to do the food shopping, leaving me with Tara and Amritsar. I cherished those few hours, in which I would chat to them, feed and play with them. I loved to rock them to sleep in my arms and sing lullabies – although Twinkle Twinkle and Rockabye Baby were my only repertoire, and even then, I couldn't remember all the words, so I just repeated the lines I knew over and over. Luckily the girls didn't seem to mind.

Even at this early stage their personalities were emerging, and I loved playing games with them. I was a very doting and slightly soppy dad.

The girls were very easy babies; they had settled into their routine and woke like clockwork, every four hours, for their feed, thanks largely to Bharti. She did insist I do some of the feeds and I was very glad of this, but it was always under her watchful eye and not the same as those delicious moments when I had the girls to myself.

Kayla wasn't coming down for a while after our arrival, and during that time I felt very much on my own. John and I spoke every day, and I longed for him to come and join us, but there was no movement from the authorities his end.

I relied on calls from family and friends to keep me sane. First among them was my mother, who phoned me once a week from Australia, where she was living. Mum was a very colourful character; interesting, amusing, and prone to exaggeration, she had always talked a lot – mostly about herself, seldom remembering to ask me about my life. But when I was in India this changed, and I saw a more understanding and empathetic side to her. She was always interested and supportive and it cheered me to know that she was on my side and rooting for me. Her calls meant a lot to me, and she kept on calling, despite complaining how high her phone bills were as a result. She also called John once a week to see how he was doing. It was thoughtful and kind of her.

Friends called too, although international calls were expensive and Skype connections were generally not good, so I often relied on emails to keep in touch. One of the friends who stayed in regular contact was Liza, an old friend from university. She had two grown-up sons of her own and loved children, so when she found out that we were becoming daddies, she was over the moon! She emailed me regularly and occasionally phoned and it always cheered me to hear from her. Without these links to John, Mum, Liza and a handful of other close friends I would have felt so much more alone and abandoned.

At night in those first weeks, I often used to go up to the roof terrace and spend time looking at the moon, huge and luminous in the clear skies of the pre-monsoon season. Up there I could be alone to watch the stars and enjoy any small breeze that broke through the heavy, hot stillness of the night.

During the day I sometimes went out to wander around Panaji, which was built on the banks of the Mandovi River and was charming, with its cobbled streets and colourful buildings.

Sometimes the nannies and I would take the babies to the nearby palm-fringed Miramar beach, but the sun was fierce, so we had to keep them in the shade. At that time of year, the beach was relatively empty and totally unspoiled. The nannies would sit under the palm trees with the babies while I swam, the water was cool, and it felt wonderful. It always amused me when we were there to see the local men running into the sea fully clothed. They seemed to enjoy it just as much as I did, despite the encumbrance of layers of clothing.

Three weeks after our arrival Kayla showed up, with her babies and her nanny, Riah. It turned out the apartment she had rented was very close to ours, which was great. After that we met up every two or three days to chat over coffee or wander down to the beach, swapping stories of our lives before babies.

Kayla ran an adult party planning business, she nicknamed Boozy Bashes and when she realised, she was going to be in India for the long haul, she ran the business from there, flying Susie, who worked with her, out to join her for a couple of weeks.

Kayla and Jamie had needed a surrogate to carry their embryos to term, but they had decided not to tell most people back in the UK what they were doing. She had me in stitches describing how she used a prosthetic stomach whilst the surrogate pregnancy progressed in India. One morning, eight months into the 'pregnancy', she heard the doorbell and rushed down to answer it, completely forgetting to put on the, by this stage, rather large prosthetic. She greeted her friend and was chatting away when she looked down and suddenly remembered. With an 'Oh Fuck!' she bolted back upstairs and strapped it on, returning minutes later as if nothing had happened. 'Tea?' she asked her rather bemused friend.

It was impossible to resist Kayla's humour and energy and she made a real difference to those long weeks in Goa. She hated to be alone, so her mother joined her for a lot of the time in Goa, friends came out for holidays with her and her father, a kind and gentle former history teacher, came to visit too.

Although Kayla and I enjoyed spending time together, sadly our nannies didn't. Bharti and Riah eyed one another with evident distaste whenever we all got together, which meant it wasn't always easy having outings with babies and nannies in tow. Kayla and I tended to meet on our own and use it as a freedom break from our domestic scenes.

Kayla and I were taking a stroll on Sinquerim Beach on June 7th, shortly after she had arrived, when she nudged me.

'Andi, look at that.'

I followed her gaze upwards.

A huge, ominous black wall of cloud could be seen to our left, moving slowly north.

'Wow, that looks...alarming.'

As we stood, transfixed, thunderclaps pealed, and lightning bolts shot across the sky.

'I guess that's the monsoon coming, then,' Kayla said.

'I guess so,' I agreed. 'Think perhaps we'd better get back home?'

We made our way hastily back to the apartment, convinced that either the world was about to end, or serious rain was on the way. We didn't have long to wait. The skies opened and the rain bucketed down in sheets, heavier than anything we'd ever witnessed back in the Home Counties. It would continue for the next four months.

Over the days that followed we got used to enormous thunderstorms. I remember rocking Tara and saying 'Thunder' as she looked up at me, seemingly unafraid of the racket going on over our heads. I stuck my tongue out and she mimicked me, making me laugh.

It didn't rain all day long, thankfully. But each day we had to wait for the deluge to finish before we ventured out and about. Goa had a special charm at this time. Almost devoid of tourists, we saw it as the locals did. It grew greener and more verdant and flowers in impossibly exotic colours bloomed everywhere.

Panaji was a peaceful town where everyone went about their business and I often went down to the fish market first thing in the morning, alongside the locals, to get some prawns or fish for us. First thing in the morning was the only time to go

– because the fish market had no refrigeration and therefore was very, very smelly. Celebrity chef Rick Stein once did a programme based in Goa and he commented on the smell in the fish market – there is, I suspect, no worse smell on the planet. As the day wore on and got hotter the fish got smellier and smellier and, of course, cheaper. But this was a bargain to avoid. The only safe fish were those straight off the boat first thing, so I was happy to pay more.

I had been in Goa for six weeks when the documents arrived from Somya. Several calls urging her politely to please get a move on had made no difference whatsoever. But eventually a package was delivered containing our surrogate Rehanna's divorce and marriage certificates and her identity card, the girls' prenatal scans and (as the obligatory six weeks had now passed) the signed and notarised document stating that Rehanna did not want to be a mother to the surrogate children, which we would also need later for our UK Parental Order.

I was hugely relieved to receive all of this. Of course, there were ridiculous fees involved, but at least we now had what we needed in order to apply for the girls' passports. Once I had checked and double-checked them, I sent all the documents to John via FedEx so that he could pass them on to the Home Office, which processed the passports in Hong Kong. Those papers would have to travel halfway around the world – I only hoped they would enable us to get the passports we needed to go home.

Beautiful as Goa was, I was all too aware that I was there simply to wait...and wait...and wait. And the waiting was hard. I missed John, missed home, missed the dogs, and felt sad about John missing out on his daughters. I couldn't help feeling that the whole, horrible delay was so unnecessary and pointless. But since there was no way around, we just had to get through it.

It was around this time that John had a bit of a tricky situation to sort out. We had agreed from the start that we would not tell anyone who the girls' biological father was. It felt like the right thing to do – they were our daughters, together, and that was all anyone needed to know. But it left John with a dilemma because he then couldn't tell his family, or anyone else, about the problems he was having with the medical visa.

He considered telling his close family the truth, but he didn't want his elderly mother to worry, so he kept it to himself and told them that all was well, he would be visiting us soon. But as time passed, he realised that he had to either fess up or somehow create a fictitious visit to us – otherwise people would begin to wonder why he wasn't coming over to see me and meet his daughters.

In the end, telling his family in Ireland and his office that he was going to India for a week, he spent a week holed up in the London flat. He let his phone battery die and after his 'return' told the office that he'd accidentally left his phone in the UK. The London neighbours were told that he was going to India the following week. So, everyone had the story that he was going to

India to meet the girls and of course they were all delighted for him.

So far so good – but that begged one important question: photos. How was he going to show them all pictures of him with Tara and Amritsar? I got a panic call from him asking me to photoshop him into some photos and send them over. I'm a dab hand with graphics, so I took some photos of me and Bharti with the girls and then cut Bharti out and put John in. The results weren't bad, except that Amritsar looked slightly larger than life and John appeared to be holding her at a slightly strange angle. I sent them over and to our amazement, no-one noticed. His family, staff and the neighbours were all just so happy that we were together, with our children, and his mother proudly showed off the photo to the rest of the family.

And how did he explain the delay in the girls getting out of India? He told everyone that the passports would take a very long time as all kinds of checks had to be done, to do with people trafficking. Which was, sort of, close to the truth.

I could hardly believe that we pulled this stunt off. It was impressive. My only worry was that keeping our troubles secret meant he had very little support his end. There was no-one he could turn to when he felt miserable. But John's way was to stay stoical and keep busy – he worked flat-out for every single day that I was in India.

I still hoped at this point that it would be straightforward from here on – get the passports, apply for the exit visas and off we would go. Kayla was in exactly the same situation and the only way we could check on progress was to call a premium phone number that cost dearly and told us nothing. You had to call, give your reference number, and hang on, only to be told that they couldn't give us any idea of when the passports would be issued. We were in limbo.

It wasn't easy for John either. He was working in London and travelling back to Berkshire every evening to look after the dogs, leaving home at 6.30am in the morning and getting back at 7pm and often later. A kind neighbour had offered to feed Remus and Gracie and let them out three times a day, but John had to be there overnight, so no matter how late work finished, he couldn't stay in the London flat.

He was still receiving blank expressions and non-committal answers from the Indian High Commission over his visa. He would arrive there with a picture of the girls, stick it on the window at the enquiry counter and say, 'These are my children, I would like to see them!' Each time someone different would come to the window and John would ask, 'Do you even know who I am?' 'Yes,' they always said. 'You are Mr Leighton'. But despite this the answer was always the same, 'You will have to wait. We have checks we must make before the visa can be issued. No, we can't tell you how long.'

John was filling his time, and working out his frustration, by decorating our new home, room by room, ready for our return. At that stage, working in the evenings and weekends, he fondly imagined that there was no way he would get through the whole house before he could join us. I only hoped he was right.

He would send me images of colour swatches so that we could choose room colours together, and then photos of his progress which was, at times, frankly chaotic. He may have been the world's best organised man at work, but as a decorator he had a way to go. The theory was fine; he even had spreadsheets of the jobs he had to do each weekend. But in practice, bored by hours of woodwork painting, John would move on to the next room, so that eventually he was midway through every room in the house. And of course, our lovable mutts didn't help. At one point, Remus walked through a tray of paint, left on the floor, and left green emulsion pawprints all over the cream carpets. John thought it was Gracie and wiped her paws, not realising that Remus was still trailing paint over the house.

At that point in time our lives couldn't have been more different. John's routine dictated by work and the dogs and his self-imposed decorating schedule, mine by nannies and the babies and waiting.

To fill the time Kayla and I took a few trips, sometimes with, sometimes without our nannies and babies. She had found a friendly taxi driver who took us to see a spice farm and an elephant sanctuary.

Then there was the time we visited the Hindu Shantadurga Temple, dedicated to Shri Shantadurga, the goddess of wealth, wisdom, and fertility.

This time we had Kayla's parents, four babies and three nannies with us. And as the day progressed, I realised I was causing something of a sensation among the local population.

Men were coming up to pat me on the back while women looked admiringly at the babies. When someone started taking photos and congratulating me the penny dropped. They all though the four babies were mine, and as the father of quads I was being elevated to the status of fertility god as I lead my entourage around. I had to laugh, especially as I wasn't biologically the father of any of the babies, which was still a source of grief.

Afterwards we went to the nearby beach and had ice cups – sweet, coloured syrup poured over ice, which Riah said reminded her of her childhood.

Occasionally we ventured further afield, to see something more of India. In mid-June we left the babies with the nannies and Kayla and her assistant Susie, and I flew up to Pune, to visit the Aga Khan's magnificent palace, built in 1892 and famed as the place where Mahatma Gandhi was imprisoned with his wife Kasturba and secretary Mahadev Desai in 1942. Gandhi was there for almost two years, during which time his wife and secretary both died. The palace was given to the nation in recognition of Gandhi and his philosophy of nonviolent resistance. Gandhi's ashes remain there, and there are memorials to him and his wife.

We walked around the exquisite gardens and spent the night in a plush hotel nearby, where we relaxed and drank cocktails and did our best to forget our frustrations with the unwieldy bureaucratic systems we were up against.

Back in Panaji it was wonderful to cuddle the girls again, and all seemed to have gone well in my absence. But a couple of mornings later I came back from an outing to the fish market to find Bharti and Geeta at opposite ends of the apartment and an atmosphere I could have cut with a knife.

Geeta had always been under Bharti's thumb. She was, I imagine, ordered to come with us on this trip to help Bharti, despite being paid only what Bharti considered her worth.
Now it emerged that Geeta had suggested Bharti go back to Mumbai, leaving Geeta to look after the babies – and to keep the wages. Bharti might have considered this, except that to allow Geeta to keep all the money was unthinkable.

The two of them were now in a stand-off. If Bharti moved, Geeta would move as far as possible from her. This went on for the next 24 hours and made life impossible, so I told Bharti quietly that perhaps it was best that Geeta should leave. It turned out that she was already booked on a bus, leaving the next day. I thanked Geeta for all she had done and slipped her an extra couple of thousand rupees, behind Bharti's back, but truth to tell I was relieved that the hostilities were over. And a few days later Bharti's mother Lalit arrived to take Geeta's place, after which, much to my relief, peace reigned in the nursery.

Chapter 7

Back to Mumbai

We had been in Panaji for several weeks when Kayla announced that she was going to move to one of the beach resorts. She told me she had found a villa. So, she and her babies, her nanny Riah, and her mother, who was still with her, moved to Candolim, half an hour's drive away.

Candolim was a small town, right on the shores of the Arabian Sea, with wide and unspoiled beaches a stone's throw away. I was beginning to look like a beach bum, with my tan and hippy T-shirts, so I decided I might feel more at home on the beach than in the city and began to think about moving there too.

Kayla's landlord was a charming British man of Indian origin, who liked to pop in for a cup of tea and a gossip with Kayla's mum. He didn't have another property for me, sadly, so I looked around and found a small apartment. I took it for a week, after which I would either stay at the beach resort or go back to Panaji.

Bharti and Lalit, the babies and I moved into the apartment. We were unpacking our cases and putting things away when I stepped into the small kitchen to get a cold drink.

As I did, I heard a cracking sound and looked down. The floor was tiled, and the tile I had stepped on must have been a bit bowed, because it had cracked. A moment later the tile next to it cracked, and then the one next to that, in a chain reaction. As I watched, horrified, the entire kitchen floor became a maze of cracking tiles, snapping, and popping like fireworks as the damage spread and pieces of tile leaped into the air and smashed back down again. In the end the whole floor had more or less exploded.

Bharti arrived and stared in amazement, shaking her head. I felt guilty, even though all I'd done was step into the room. It was an unfortunate accident, no-one's fault (except perhaps the chap who laid the tiles). But the whole floor would have to be replaced so we clearly couldn't stay there.

Bharti's son was visiting for a holiday, although not staying with us, so he went to get pizza for supper, because we couldn't use the kitchen to cook with the floor in shreds. At Bharti's urging I phoned Ramesh, the owner of the apartment we'd rented in Panaji. He had a villa in Candolim, and it was free for the next few weeks. It was expensive compared to the apartment, but we needed a refuge and two days later we moved. Ramesh was waiting there for us, I had to pay him in cash, and as I counted out the piles of rupees he sat, his eyes fixed on the money, literally rubbing his hands together in glee. A performance of such blatant greed that I didn't know whether to laugh or feel offended.

The villa was much bigger than what became known as the 'exploding tile apartment' so we enjoyed the space and settled down for a couple of weeks at the seaside. Candolim beach was wide and unspoiled and during the days that followed Kayla and I explored all the other beaches in the area. We enjoyed the laid-back beach bars on Sinquerim and the hippy chill style of Baga, avoided the lager-lout vibe of Calangute (although there were few tourists around at that time) and finally agreeing that our favourite was Anjuna, north of Baga and still a fairly hippy place, with a beach bar where we would enjoy an ice-cold bottle of Indian Kingfisher lager. It was one of the few beach bars that remained open even in the off season. It tended to be frequented by uber-chilled expats and it wasn't unusual to meet one of them relaxing there with a joint in one hand and a beer in the other.

All of the beaches were the haunt of small crowds of local children, many of them begging or offering wares for sale or to give the tourists manicures. Kayla would pay one to do her nails, and end up with dozens around her, all hoping for a few rupees.

Throughout this time, I had the strange feeling that life was on hold. I was still just waiting, and nothing appeared to be happening. I would make my daily call to John in the afternoon – morning for him – and discuss options and possibilities, fanning the flames of hope, but in reality, there was no option but to wait.

In the evenings I would sit on the villa's veranda watching the night sky, the stars and moon no longer visible behind the blanket of the monsoon's low cloud. I would picture John watching the same moon almost five thousand miles away and wonder how long it would be until I could take the girls home to him.

To pass the time Kayla and I took another short trip, this time to Delhi for the weekend. She had found us a house to rent, so off we went to see the Taj Mahal. And yes, I sat on the bench where Princess Diana had sat in the famous photo, looking so reflective, and yes, I did ponder for a while on where I was and what our future would hold.

I was still very keen to be biological father to a child. I had already been in touch with Doran, the Israeli we had met at the Lakeside Apartments. He worked for Tammuz, a surrogate agency, and he said that he could arrange a surrogate for me in Bangkok, Thailand. India was now out of the question, after the legal clamp-down on surrogacies, but Thailand was still in business.

Doran worked regularly with the South African organisation whose egg-donors had been staying at the Lakeside when we were there. He suggested I get in touch to arrange for an egg donor.

I found their website and saw Sophie's name on the contact list. She and her girlfriend Lauren had been at Lakeside, where Lauren was mother hen to the group of women there to make egg deposits. Sophie had been a nice woman, very caring and friendly. I hoped she would remember me. I emailed her to say hello and she replied almost instantly, asking how I was and how the girls were doing. I replied that we were all well and asked her for the password to the website. Once I had logged on, I scanned the faces – and very quickly recognised Rene.

I told Sophie I would love to attempt another pregnancy, with Rene as egg donor. She said that could be arranged and recommended a clinic in Thailand. She said she was often there for egg-retrieval with the egg donors, and she could meet me there in mid-August. I contacted the clinic and booked an appointment and so the plan was set. I was delighted. India might have closed its doors to us, but Thailand had not – I still had the chance of fathering a child.

In early July I was notified that I would be required to go for an interview with the British Consulate in Mumbai. They also wanted to see the girls' surrogate, Rehanna. None of this was necessary for the passports to be issued, but I was told that we had been randomly selected for interview. Who knows whether this was true? I wasn't particularly keen to meet Rehanna, but we would have to go for interview together, so I had no choice.

A couple of weeks later we headed back to Mumbai, hopeful that, once this interview was completed, the passports would be issued. Kayla went too, as the waiting period for passports was, theoretically, over, and although there was no word from the authorities, she too was hoping they would soon be through. As we both made travel plans and packed up our Goan houses, I was painfully aware that all the new parents of other nationalities that we had met at Lakeside would have long since returned home, their children with them, able to carry on with their family lives. Only the British – Kayla and I – were still there, still waiting. Our presence, and no doubt that of other Brits in the same situation, was a shaming indictment of our government and its slow, heartless, and unnecessary procedures.

Kayla decided we would all move into a nice apartment in Mumbai together for the next couple of weeks. She flew back, but Bharti's mother was too frightened to fly, so I had to hire a car and we drove the 700 miles back. Bharti's husband Sanjay had come down to join us, and he drove the car, with me beside him in the front and Bharti and her mother with the girls in the back. We set off at 6am and finally reached Mumbai at 8 that evening. The journey was picturesque, we passed paddy fields and villages and some stunning mountain scenery, but inevitably it all began to blur as the hours passed and by the time, we had been on the road for 14 hours, all we wanted was to eat and sleep.

Apart from loo breaks we'd only stopped once for a meal, but at that stop I had a special moment with Tara. Holding her I began making baby noises – ooh, ahh, boo, boo when she suddenly replied, with a perfect imitation of ooh, ahh. I grinned; my little girl was starting to talk! 'Very good talking to you

Booboo' I said. And from that moment on she became Booboo and Amritsar was Baabaa.

Kayla, her babies and her parents were all installed in the apartment – in a building called the Oberoi Splendour – when we arrived. Bharti and her mother went home with Sanjay, the girls and I settled into our cool and stylish apartment and after that Bharti would come each day to look after the children. As a second nanny, this time she brought her daughter-in-law Priti, daughter of Geeta, to help her look after all four children.

Soon after we arrived, I went for my interview at the British Consulate. With Bharti and Tara and Amritsar in tow, I set off in a Rickshaw, which then went around in circles for some time before we found the Consulate in the middle of a business park in central Mumbai.

When we got there, Bharti was refused entry and told by security guards to wait outside, while I went in with the girls. The two officials who greeted us were called Daisy and Zubin, they seemed pleasant and chatted as they escorted me to a small waiting room.

Somya had arranged for Rehanna to join us there, and as I sat and waited for her, a baby in a car seat on either side of me, I was full of apprehension. Meeting at all had not figured in our plans, and nor had allowing her to see the girls again. We had paid her well for her services, the equivalent of four years' income in a good job, and we had believed that was an end to her role. Now here I was, sitting in a grim, sixties-style office with a bare wooden table and plastic chairs, waiting to meet her.

Minutes later she was ushered in by Zubin. Rehanna, who was wearing a sari, came over to me and the girls. She reached out to pick up Tara, who screamed, so she turned instead to Amritsar. There was nothing tender or motherly about Rehanna's interaction with the girls, I could see that she felt no special connection with them and this I found reassuring. I said thank you to her in the local language, Maharati, for what she had done for us, and she smiled.

Zubin, whose name I recognised as someone who had already been in touch with Kayla over her application, was very friendly. He showed us to a cubicle and introduced us to the British Consular official who had come down from Delhi to conduct the interview. It was straightforward, a list of standard official questions, and soon over, after which we were shown back downstairs to where Bharti was waiting. She took one of the car seats from me and muttered, 'Mr Andi you must give Rehanna some travel money.' Startled, I fumbled for 2000 rupees, around £20, and gave it to Rehanna, who thanked me and then left. I hoped, fervently, that we would not need to meet again. A hope that would soon turn out to be foolishly naive.

A couple of days later I made a flying trip to Bangkok to visit the All-IVF Clinic there and make my deposit. Sophie was there to meet me and the staff there, admin assistant Nancy and a nurse called Natmanee, were welcoming and efficient. Sophie told me they would attempt a pregnancy immediately, before the sperm was frozen, as that might give the best chance and I couldn't help but be excited.

I did wonder if I was being selfish. After all, we had two healthy daughters. But I couldn't help longing for a child that would have my DNA. John and I had agreed we would gladly have three or even four children. I refused to let myself think about the potential problems in getting any future children back to the UK, the problems we were having in India were largely a result of the change in the surrogacy law and in any other country it would be far more straightforward. We had simply come at the wrong time, it was bad luck, but it couldn't happen again.

I was in Bangkok for just two nights, having left the girls with Kayla and her parents and the nannies. I would hear within two or three weeks whether the attempted pregnancy had been successful, so I left Thailand filled with anticipation and hope.

When I returned to India, I discovered that the passports for Kayla's children, Millie, and Max, had arrived. Kayla was euphoric and I couldn't help but be happy for her. At the same time, I wondered why her passports had come through, with no need for an interview, while mine had been held up. Was there something I didn't know? Or was I just being paranoid. That day I came close to tears. Would Kayla soon be off home, leaving me on my own in India?

I didn't have much time to brood on this because we had trouble at the apartment. Our landlord had discovered that the nannies sometimes stayed the night and he erupted with fury, demanding a lot more money and screaming at us so aggressively that Kayla's father, Daniel was shaking and close to collapse, his hand on his chest. I was alarmed, and I had to insist that the landlord leave and stop frightening an elderly couple. He backed off, but he did not give up and in the end, we decided to leave after only 12 days. Kayla, with her parents and babies, went back to the Lakeside Apartments. I couldn't afford to go with her, so I rented another apartment across the road from the one we were in, in a building called the Lalco Residency. While it was a stone's throw from the Oberoi Splendor, inside it could have been on another planet. The apartment was dated, with flaky paint on the walls, dreary lino floors and bars over the windows. Added to that we were right over a road that was heavy with traffic, the drone was loud and the pollution dense and smelly. And the young boys who came to mop the floors used filthy water. We had to ask them to go and find some clean water, or not to do the floors. I hated it and I hoped, passionately, that we wouldn't have to stay there for long.

Within days Kayla called to say she had got her children's exit visas. She had been advised by her lawyer in India to use an agent, a third party who, for a significant fee, could talk to the right people and speed things up. She had been asked for additional documents by the Foreigners Regional Registration Office (FRRO) and Daisy from the British Consulate in Mumbai had supplied them, at which point the FRRO granted the visas. Kayla was on her way, and I was going to miss her.

On Kayla's last night in India, I went out for a meal with her and her parents. We ended it with hugs and tears and when I got into my rickshaw to go back to the Lalco Apartments I felt very dejected indeed. How long was it going to be for me and our girls?

The following day I called John, who said he had good news.

'Remember that Spanish au pair my sister used to have?' he said. 'She was called Manuela and she was great with the kids?'

I did remember, vaguely. I had met her in London when she had stayed with us in our apartment. I recalled that she liked football and Martina Navratilova. She also liked to speak her mind and had been rather opinionated, but it was true that she was very good with John's sister's children.

'Well,' John went on. 'I've been in touch with her, she's free at the moment and I've hired her to come out and help you. I thought it would cheer you up to have a friendly face there with you.'

I knew John was doing his best to make up for the fact that he couldn't be there with me. And perhaps he was right; Manuela might be good company and help to fill the void that Kayla and her family had left.

A week later I went to the airport to meet Manuela's plane. I spotted her across the concourse, before she saw me. A tall, fair-haired and heavily built woman, she stood out among the crowd as she made her way through, looking nervously around for me.

I thought that Manuela would make life easier over the coming weeks. More than anything, of course, I hoped we wouldn't be in India too much longer. By the time she arrived it had already been almost five months. So, it was reasonable to expect that it could only be another few weeks at most. And with Manuela to keep me and the girl's company those weeks would fly by.

Except that, unfortunately, things did not go smoothly with Manuela, almost from the start. She was dismayed by the apartment, the heat, the crowds, and the food. She insisted she must work only an eight-hour day and then stop, so that everything had to be fitted around this. She wanted to take the babies out, and I wasn't keen, because of the crowded, dusty, dirty artery of a road we lived on. It was the through road to the slum areas, so the rickshaw drivers all went that way to get home, and they would regularly stop and defecate at the side of the road, when the urge took them. So, walking anywhere was hazardous to say the least.

For a short while Manuela did her shift during the day, while Bharti came to look after the babies in the evening and at night. This arrangement bumped along reasonably well – until

Manuela accused Bharti of theft. I suspect Bharti was probably stuffing a couple of the babies' disposable nappies into her bag for her grandson. And honestly, I would have been happy to overlook it, Bharti had been a wonderful help to me for several months and I needed her. But once Manuela, trembling with indignation, loudly voiced her accusations, that was it – Bharti was off.

'I cannot stay here with this woman Mr Andi,' she said, her voice filled with outrage. 'I love you like family. Amritsar and Tara are my beautiful girls, but that woman is BAD.'

What to do? I would rather have had Bharti than Manuela, but I had no choice. Bharti left that day. I was heartbroken. I had been genuinely fond of Bharti, who managed the girls with calm efficiency and had been a great support. Her departure left Manuela, with her eight-hour day, and me, with the girls for the other 16 hours, both sharing the small apartment and neither of us very happy about it. I was concerned about Tara and Amritsar too. They had become used to Bharti and the unsettled atmosphere could not be good for them.

Over the next few days both Manuela and I suffered from upset stomachs. And she was convinced it was my cooking. The apartment was not particularly clean, it always smelled rather musty. The apartment was serviced by young Indian boys who cleaned were enthusiastic and thorough, but they used the same bowl of water for the whole apartment block, rinsing their cloths in increasingly filthy water as they worked their way round.

Because of this I was very careful about food preparation, never putting the food directly onto the counters and washing utensils very carefully. I knew the food was not picking up dirt. But the meals I made were Indian, and this didn't suit Manuela.

Actually, nothing about India suited Manuela. She would go off on solo tourist trips, disappearing for hours and then arriving back in tears because she felt that everyone had tried to rip her off and treat her like an idiot. She thought of herself as a tough woman and a feminist and being taken for a fool, as she saw it, didn't fit with this. I tried to explain to her that India was a country where women were second class citizens and where, with such widespread poverty, everyone was keen to make money and tourists were often seen as easy prey.

I did sympathise. She felt uncomfortable and unable to find her footing and it was perhaps not surprising. India was a different world, and it took a lot of adjusting to settle into life there, especially in the apartment where we were living.

Still determined to take the girls out Manuela tried to get me to buy a double buggy so that she could walk the babies to a park. Except that there wasn't a 'park'. There was a small play area in the next-door apartment complex, with two broken swings and a derailed roundabout. And despite Manuela's repeated requests, I was not about to let her disappear out with the girls, the three of them totally vulnerable. In the end, exasperated, I shouted at her, 'This is the bloody Jogeshwari Link

Road, not a leafy park in London. The babies are not leaving this apartment.'

By late August I had been in India for five months and I was staving off moments of near despair. Kayla had gone, Bharti had gone, Manuela was a nightmare and John was no closer to getting his visa... and then John called to tell me that the girls' passports had arrived.

Chapter 8

Desperate Times

John sent me the passports by FedEx and with their arrival I dared to believe that we might soon be going home. I called John to say I had them and the two of us were close to tears with relief. It had been a long, hard, wait, but it was surely now almost over.

All we had to do was to obtain the girls' exit visas. This had been fairly straightforward for Kayla. I could only hope, after the setbacks we'd already encountered, that our luck would hold, and it would be equally straightforward for us. I knew that Kayla had used an agent, but at that stage, having spent so much already, I was reluctant to pay out any more money than necessary. Besides which I believed that it should be perfectly straightforward getting the exit visas myself. A notion that turned out to be hopelessly wide of the mark, but I wasn't to discover that until much later.

I needed to make a visit to the FRRO, the Foreigner Regional Registration Offices, to request the visas. The FRRO was in the south of the city, a good hour's taxi ride from our apartment. The day after the passports arrived, I called Ram, a friendly taxi driver I had often used before, and we set off with

Manuela and the girls in their car seats. Kayla had confirmed what I would need, and I had all the necessary documents with me, many of them the same ones we had needed for the passport applications – birth certificates, surrogacy agreement, hospital summary and letters from the hospital, Somya's clinic and our landlord, saying that everything had been paid in full. It had taken a lot of work to get it all together, but now it was all there and all in order. And yet, as we navigate the dense Mumbai traffic, I couldn't help feeling nervous.

The FRRO turned out to be a rather dilapidated former colonial building, full of long corridors lines with linoleum tiling and uncomfortable metal benches and with old-fashioned ceiling fans providing the only, totally ineffectual, cooling system. I sat Manuela and the girls on a bench and joined the inevitable queue. It was long and slow, and it was almost lunchtime by the time I reached the front. I explained to the woman sitting at the reception desk, why we were there. She asked me to wait. Minutes later an official came out of the door behind her, and she directed him to me.

'What do you want?' he asked abruptly.

'I need exit visas for my daughters, Tara and Amritsar,' I replied.

'You are the father?' he asked.

'No, well, not exactly. My partner is the biological father, but he is still waiting for a medical visa to come into the country.

I have power of attorney; I am their legal guardian, and I am his next of kin. And the children's other parent.'

The official, who I learned was called Mr Rodriguez, looked unmoved.

'The father should have got a tourist visa. We would have fined him 60 US dollars. You have been badly advised.'

By-passing the irony of an Indian government official telling me that we had been badly advised to follow official recommendations and should have simply opted for deception, I took a deep breath and tried again.

'Yes, I understand that now, but we did not know that when we applied for our visas. So now the children's father is in London, unable to get a visa, and I am here with them. They have their passports; we simply need exit visas so that I can take them home.'

Mr Rodriguez eyed me with disdain. 'No father here, no visas,' he said.

I had to fight hard to stay calm. 'What can I do to get the visas? I have already been here for five months. Please tell me how we can get the visas?'

Mr Rodriguez shrugged. 'I can't help you.' And he walked back through the door and disappeared.

At this point all the waiting and frustration of the past five months hit me with full force. I had thought we were almost home and dry, but it looked as though we had come up against a brick wall. I felt my knees might give way.

I went back to find Manuela and the babies, both of whom were fast asleep. Manuela looked alarmed when she saw my face.

'What happened?'

'The dratted visas have been refused. They won't issue them unless John is here. And as you know John can't get here. We are in a Catch 22 situation.'

'What is Catch 22 situation?' Manuela asked.

'It's when you're caught in a loop of craziness. A situation you can't escape from because of crazy rules.'

She looked baffled.

'It was a book,' I said. 'And it became a term for, well this kind of situation.' She didn't look any more enlightened. 'Never mind,' I said. 'Let's go home.'

We found Ram and his slightly battered Ford sitting outside waiting for us. Once we were all in the car, he turned to me.

'All good Mr Andi? You have visas?'

'All not good Ram,' I said. 'We do not have visas and we don't know how to get them.' I burst into tears.

Ram did the head wobble as he navigated the traffic. 'India red tape not good,' he said. 'I am sorry Mr Andi. Do not lose heart. You will find a way; I am sure of this.'

'I really hope so Ram,' I sobbed. 'Otherwise, we are going to be here indefinitely.'

For the rest of the journey, I stared gloomily out of the window at the dusty lines of traffic and the crowds jostling their way along the street. What on earth was I going to do now?'

Back in the apartment I called John, who was horrified. 'There's got to be a way,' he said. 'Don't worry Andi, I'll try everything I can from this end.'

That night I couldn't sleep and when I did finally drift into an uneasy doze before dawn, I had nightmares about being trapped and unable to breathe.

The next morning, exhausted and demoralised, I sat down to try to think about what I could do. There had to be a way – or was I going to be in India forever? Perhaps if I just went back and pleaded some more. I pictured Mr Rodriguez stony face. Perhaps not.

That day, September 5th, it was announced that the illustrious and very elderly, in fact 96-year-old, Dr Lakhumal Hiranandani had died. This was the man after whom the hospital where the girls were born had been named. Both a doctor and a property dealer, he had been fabulously wealthy; two of his sons still feature on the list of India's wealthiest 100 people. When his death was announced everything stopped, the entire community went into mourning and posters appeared in the local supermarket paying homage to him. I found this odd, but Indians idolise the very rich and his hospital was well-known, despite the fact that most local residents could never have afforded to be treated there. Rumours circulated among the expat community that the Hiranandani family had been involved in a huge amount of corruption. Since I had got to know one man who had actually worked for the family and left in disgust at their dealings, I didn't doubt it. But to the poorer residents of the city, unaware of anything other than the doctor's well-publicised philanthropy, he was a god-like figure.

Meanwhile I had problems of my own. In addition to the quandary of how to get the exit visas, I was struggling to manage the childcare with only Manuela to help. The girls seemed far more unsettled than they had been in Goa under Bharti's calm and ordered regime. I was often up at night with one or both of them crying and I needed more help than Manuela was willing to give. In addition, I was clearly going to have to get out and about trying to sort the visa situation. I decided that I had to find another nanny.

There was no chance that Bharti would come back as long as Manuela was there, so I asked Faskia, the friendly and rather flirtatious girl on the reception desk at the flats if she knew of a good nanny. Faskia loved to chat and, I had a suspicion that she fancied me.

'Oh Mr Andrew, I will find you a good nanny,' she told me, beaming. An hour later she gave me the number of a woman named Manju whose previous employers had just gone back to Australia. I called her, and she arrived the following day with a friend in tow. Middle-aged and pleasant, Manju seemed like just what we needed. I hired her on the spot, and she agreed to start immediately and I agreed that her cousin Nikki, younger and quieter than Manju, could help us with some night shifts.

I told Manuela that I had hired a nanny – two nannies. I was prepared for objections and prepared to counter them. But what she said was, 'I've been thinking of going back to the UK for a break, just for a week or so. I haven't been feeling well.'

I knew she had been miserable; in fact, I had begun to worry that she was heading for a breakdown. And with her lack of insight into the Indian culture and her union-style demands for set hours, she was anything but the helpful companion I had hoped for. But she was also all I had, and I didn't want to feel completely alone. I agreed that she should go back for a break, just for a week or two. It might do us both good.

I packed most of my clothes for Manuela to take back. I was determined that, one way or another, the girls and I would be going home soon, and I'd collected far too much stuff. So, keeping only a couple of changes of clothing, I sent it all with her.

When Manuela had left, I felt desolate again. Everyone, it seemed could go home, except me. All the couples I had met who were in India for surrogate babies had left. Only recently I'd said goodbye to a very likeable couple I had met, Norwegians Torgeir (pronounced Torgay and known most of the time as Tor) and Kjertil Andersson because they were fellow residents in the Lalco apartments. Torgeir and I got chatting in the corridor one day and I invited him in to meet the girls. He was completely soppy over them, he thought they were wonderful. He told me he was there with his partner as their daughter was due the next day. The door was still open, and his partner Kjertil followed him in a few minutes later. We chatted for a bit and then they said, 'We're off for a cigarette in the spare room. Want to come?' I did, it was so nice to meet fellow secret smokers. They puffed away with their windows wide open, and the door closed. 'We're not going down eight flights of stairs every time we smoke a cigarette,' Torgeir laughed. 'We smoke too much.'

It turned out that they had also used the Rotunda Clinic and their baby's conception had taken place well after the rule-change banning surrogate births for same-sex couples, so the clinic had clearly just carried on. They told me that, after a series of errors, not necessarily hers, Somya had been ousted from the Rotunda.

They were wild with excitement when their daughter, Aria, arrived a day later, and a few days after that they brought her home and it was my turn to be soppy. I'd already forgotten how tiny new-borns were! Over the next few weeks, we became good friends. Torgeir, known as Tor, always made me smile, he was a lovely man. After they left, their daughter's passport through in a matter of weeks, I felt more bereft than ever.

Trawling Facebook one day I came across Kari Ann Volden, a Norwegian woman who had been stranded in India for 18 months with her twins. I got in touch, and she told me her story. She had used an Indian surrogate to give birth using donated egg and sperm and her twin boys were born in early

2010. But Norway had refused to issue passports for Kari Ann to take them home, insisting that the surrogate was their mother. India took the same stance. Kari Ann had eventually managed to get the children back to Norway, after an eighteen-month battle, and she had legally adopted them there. Her case had caused an outcry since the babies were effectively stateless for 18 months. There had even been a documentary about what happened to her and her children.

Could that happen to us, I wondered? Kari Ann had only got out of India a year before our girls were born. My heart sank. I could only pray that it didn't.

In Manuela's absence Manju and Nikki settled into a routine, with Nikki working during the day and Manju at night. This system worked well; the babies had a more settled routine, and we all got more sleep.

Initially I got to know Nikki better, as she was there during the day. In her late twenties, she spoke good English and was cheerful and chatty. Like Manju, she always dressed in brightly coloured saris. They referred to one another as cousins, but I don't think they were related. Both of them used to sing to the girls – Nikki opted for Bollywood pop songs which she sang in a very sweet, melodic voice. Manju's choices were old Hindu songs that she warbled in a scratchy register, the effect of which made your blood run cold.

Manju turned out to be a bit of a battle-axe, a strong woman who was outspoken and, at times, even fierce. Added to which, I discovered that she had once been Bharti's friend, but they had fallen out and were now arch rivals. Bharti would no-doubt know, through the network they all belonged to, that Manju had come to work for us, and would not be happy. But what could I do?

Shortly after Manuela left Manju came to talk to me.

'Mr Andi,' she said. 'You are very worried; I can see that. And I want to help. I have a guru; he is very holy, and he is taking away all my troubles. This too can be you. Take this book and write down the word ram many times, 100 times, on every page. This is what you have to do, and it will help you.'

'Really?' I was desperate, and I could see she was trying to help, but was this honestly the answer to my troubles?

'Yes, really,' Manju nodded vigorously. 'I am doing this and all things in my life are good. It is a form of meditation; you will find peace while doing this and you will find strength. Troubles will go.'

What can I say? It's indicative of how hopeless I felt that I didn't dismiss what Manju said. I took the book, thanked her and began writing the word 'Ram' over and over on every page. And I kept it up over the next couple of weeks. If nothing else, it distracted me. But sadly, it didn't lead to the melting away of all my troubles. In fact, quite the opposite. I thought things were already grim, but over the following two weeks, they got far, far worse.

First of all, I heard that the attempt at creating a pregnancy in Thailand had failed. It was an awful blow, and convinced me, if I needed convincing further, that I was not capable of fathering a child. I felt inconsolable.

Then John told me that Manuela, who was staying in our London flat, had decided she could not come back to India. She had had enough, and she was ditching me, and our girls. I felt let down and angry.

Finally, I realised that my own Indian visa, granted back in March for six months, was about to run out. If I didn't manage to get it extended, who was going to stay with the girls? It was unthinkable.

Weighed down with troubles, I felt close to rock bottom. Concerned about my mental state, I asked Faskia to call a doctor. A couple of hours later a round-bellied middle-aged Indian family doctor arrived at my door. He came in and sat down and asked me, kindly, what was going on. I told him the whole story, and, with real concern, he offered to write a letter for the authorities, stating that I was suffering from depression and that I should be considered for early assistance at the visa office. I was grateful, and although I thought it unlikely that it would help, it was worth a try.

He left me with a prescription for Diazepam, an antidepressant. Later on, I took it to the pharmacy and was told that it could not be filled for me. Local pharmacies were not allowed to give members of the public drugs like these, even on prescription. I would have needed to go to a hospital pharmacy to get it filled.

When his letter arrived, a couple of days later, I did forward it to the FRRO, but of course it made no difference at all.

John and my mother both gave me all the support they could. But in the end, I had to find a way out of the mess I was in. And as I contemplated my next move, I realised that I had all the motivation I needed in the girls. Tara and Amritsar, almost six months old now, sitting up and even starting to crawl, plump with baby curves, smiling, chuckling, and chattering away in oohs and aahs, meant the world to me. I was a parent now and that had changed everything. They were mine and I was theirs and I would never, ever let them down. So whatever troubles came my way, I would just have to get on with things.

'One way and another,' I told them, as they stared at me with huge, trusting eyes, 'we are going home. Your Daddy John is waiting for us, and we are going to have a wonderful life together, the four of us.'

The following day I got Ram to drive me to the British Consulate where I had an appointment with Zubin, the official I had met when I went for the interview a few weeks earlier. Zubin, previously all smiles, told me solemnly that unfortunately there was nothing the Consulate could do for me. 'It's all in the hands of the FRRO,' he explained helpfully.

So, back to see Mr Rodriguez. After another morning spent queuing, he extended my visa by six days. 'You will have to come back every six days for another extension,' he said, his face deadpan. I asked him if there was any possible movement on the girls' exit visas. 'No,' he replied. 'The father must come.'

I was now in India at the whim of the FRRO and I would need an exit visa myself in order to go home. I had no legal right to be in India, other than my guardianship of the girls. My situation felt precarious, to say the least.

In London John redoubled his efforts with the Indian High Commission, explaining to them just how difficult things were for us. What could possibly justify their withholding his visa? And yet they continued to give him noncommittal answers.

It was, by this time, the end of September. I was tied into making the trek to the FRRO every six days – and holding my breath with anxiety every time until I got the next extension – and we had absolutely no way to get the girls' visas. And then, in another strange development, Rehanna, our surrogate, turned up, out of the blue. She had tracked me down – not hard, I suppose, with the nanny network – and she said that she wanted to see the girls. I was pretty sure she did not, it had to be cash she was after. But I did not dare send her away empty-handed. With my situation so precarious, I might just need her. I gave her 10,000 rupees, the equivalent of £100, and off she went.

This was the start of her regular visits. The following week she was back again, this time with her brother. The next time she brought her two children so that Tara and Amritsar could meet 'their brother and sister'. I wasn't happy; Tara and

Amritsar were not actually related to Rehanna and her children at all. She was simply milking the situation for all she could get. Each time she came I let her in for a few minutes and then gave her some money, ushering her out of the door as fast as possible.

Tara never seemed to take to Rehanna, and she always crawled back to me when Rehanna approached her, but Amritsar was fascinated by Rehanna's bangles and her brightly coloured sari. I had to resist the impulse to carry Amritsar off, as Rehanna literally banked on this affection by milking me for more cash. And when her other excuses ran dry, she would tell me that her mother was sick and needed medicines. Through gritted teeth I paid up, reminding myself that diplomacy was more important than anything at this stage.

One evening Manju arrived looking excited. 'Mr Andi,' she said. 'I want to help you. And it is possible that I can. I know of a lawyer, Pratik. I think you should go and see him and ask whether he can mediate for you to get your exit visas.'

I thanked her, and immediately rang the number she gave me for Pratik. Any lead was better than none. Pratik told me to come and see him the following day. I needed to go back to the FRRO for another visa extension that day too, so I asked Ram to do the round trip to Pratik's office and on to our now regular haunt, the FRRO.

Ram and I had become good friends, due to the not inconsiderable amount of time I spent in his taxi. He had adopted the attitude of a big brother, asking me, with filial concern, how

I was and often stopping on our journeys so that we could have a samosa or a cup of sweet tea. I was fond of him and always glad of his cheery presence as we navigated the complex traffic arteries of the city. He sometimes sang old Hindu songs to me as we drove, his high-pitched, reedy voice reminding me of Bharti's when she had sung Bollywood songs to the girls to send them to sleep.

Pratik told me that he knew of a 'man on the inside' named Shashi, who could organise our visas. I naturally assumed he meant on the inside of the FRRO. This was heartening news. It would cost us, of course it would, but by this time I would have taken out a second mortgage if I had to in order to get out of India. Pratik told me that Shashi would need an extra document, tying in my relationship to John, since no-one accepted our civil partnership certificate. Apparently, this new document had to come from the British Consulate, so I promised to visit them to get it.

I headed down to the British Consulate a day later and managed to see Zubin, who told me that they were not there to produce random documents for the FRRO at a whim.

'Hardly a whim,' I told him. 'Getting my children home to England depends on this. Surely you could help?'

That would be a no. Zubin could not help. I tried Daisy, the other official I knew in the Consulate. I was sure she had supplied Kayla with something similar, as Kayla and Jamie had not been married. Daisy told me firmly that it was none of my business how she had assisted Kayla – the fact was that I was not going to be given any assistance by her or Zubin. The document would not be produced.

It seemed that wherever I turned, doors were slammed in my face. Every time there was a chink of hope, it was snuffed out by some cold-blooded, obdurate bureaucrat, without humanity and impervious to our very difficult situation, even though two small children were involved.

I called John, who could hear the desperation in my voice. He said he had found a Foreign Office contact, through a neighbour, and he would try that route to speed up the arrival of his medical visa. But a couple of days later he reported back that the contact had asked one of his staff to phone the Indian High Commission. The staff member had simply called the general helpline number and had reported back that it was engaged. Which the contact guy duly reported back to John. And that appeared to be that.

Pratik, the lawyer, insisted I must get the document or the FRRO would not allow the babies to leave. Back I went to the Consulate, where Zubin, furious that I was still trying to get him to help, called Daisy. 'Who wants this document?' she asked. I told him it was someone called Shashi, who I believed worked for the FRRO. Daisy rang the FRRO and was told that no-one named Shashi worked there. When this was relayed back to me, I was shocked. Had Pratik lied to me? Did Shashi not exist?

Once again, I was sent away from the British Consulate with nothing. And they made it very clear that I wasn't to bother them again. Heartless didn't seem a strong enough term. How hard would it have been for them to simply get me the document?

When I returned to the FRRO for my next visa extension I was confronted by a furious Mr Rodriguez. He was not at all happy that the British Embassy had called and spoken to his superiors about this 'Mr Shashi'. It was at that point that I understood – far from being an FRRO staff member, Shashi was an 'agent', a fixer, who would lubricate the passage of the exit visas with a healthy bribe to the staff. Mr Rodriguez was angry because my blunder in thinking that Shashi worked for the FRRO had almost exposed the entire 'agent' system, the fruits of which some of those working there enjoyed.

I had made a mistake that cost me dear. Had I realised that Shashi was an agent, I would never have mentioned him. Now I was in trouble with the British and with the Indians. Absolutely no-one had any interest in helping me. I had been cut adrift, with no idea how I was ever going to get our girls home.

Chapter 9

<u>Breakthrough</u>

Our apartment was just too expensive. As time went on the costs involved with the two nannies as well as me and the girls was mounting. With no idea when we would be leaving India, we couldn't stay in the Lalco building for much longer.

Manju came to the rescue, by telling me that a friend of hers would rent us a modest flat in central Powai. We moved the following week, much to the disappointment of Faskia, in the Lalco reception, who said she would miss us, hugged me and gave me her email address. I told her we'd miss her too and thanked her for everything she'd done for us.

The small two-bedroom flat Manju took us to was tucked down a narrow side street. Inside it seemed, if not exactly luxurious, then comfortable enough. That is, until a couple of days later the drains flooded. Within a week we realised that this was not a one-off, it was happening all the time. The sanitation system was totally inadequate, the flat smelled awful and to make things worse the young boy who slept on the balcony and did the cleaning actually did very little. He would chat to the nannies and then wander off. Perhaps because he was paid so badly by the landlord.

Our side street was off a main road. Traffic was heavy, but at least we were not directly over the road, as we had been in the previous apartment. The trouble was, walking back up the street I kept falling into the potholes, and some of them were deep. Navigating my way down the smelly, hole-filled street, I hoped fervently that we wouldn't have to be there for too long.

In the evenings, before the cleaning boy went to sleep out there, I would step onto the balcony for a cigarette. It overlooked a car park, next to which was a building site with some kind of building which appeared to have been abandoned in the early stages. Perhaps the builders had run out of money. Around the car park and the site there was a pack of street dogs, perhaps 19 or 20 of them, running wild and barking incessantly. These dogs were everywhere in Mumbai, no-one could afford to keep or feed them and with so many people struggling to survive, dog-rescue was hardly anyone's priority. The dogs just roamed the streets, lean and hungry and noisy.

On the building site there was a security guard. One lunchtime as I stood smoking, I saw him drag an old wooden chair from his small hut close to the electric gate and then disappear back inside to emerge with a glass of water. As I watched he purred it on the tarmac in front of the chair and then he sat and stared at the pool of water.

I disappeared back inside to play with Amritsar and Tara for a while. When I returned to the balcony the guard was still there, staring at the pool, which had shrunk to maybe half its size. I went back inside and half an hour later I returned for a cigarette. He was still sitting their staring at the pool of water, now very small. By the time I had finished my cigarette the stain of water was all but gone. The guard got up out of his chair and disappeared into his hut, returning moments later with a very large stick. He stomped out of the gate and into the building site and started lashing out at the dogs, which were barking and running everywhere, swinging his stick as he went. He shouted something intelligible and continued to thrash his stick at the dogs for a while. A few minutes later he calmly put his stick down and walked back to his chair on the tarmac, where he sat and looked into space.

This sad scene haunted me. I felt the guard, there day after day for what would have been a pittance, ignored, under-valued and with nothing to do, must have felt his soul was destroyed, to the point where all he could find to do was to watch water evaporate. It made me question my own value in the greater scheme of things. I felt pretty broken myself but watching the guard I realised that there are always those so much worse off.

It was on that same balcony that I stood and watched the moon. The monsoon was in retreat by this time and the moon was clear again; luminous and golden. It always comforted me to see it, knowing that at home John could see it too.

There had been seven full moons since I arrived in India, and I still had no idea how we were going to get home. Mr

Rodriguez, it seemed, had a general dislike of the British and an acute loathing for me in particular. He had warned every agent who did business with the FRRO that I was to be avoided at all costs. So now that I finally understood I needed an agent, I could not find one.

An agent, I now knew, could by-pass the long queues that formed daily at the reception desk in the FRRO by going straight to the other side of reception. Here there was another corridor and a couple of rooms where the agents and the FRRO staff would do 'business'. And then, lo and behold, you would find your paperwork processed. Kayla told me that it had cost her £150 for an agent to speed up her children's visa application. Plus, the agent's fee. She had gone to the FRRO with the agent and voila, all the boxes had been ticked and she was free to go – and to take her children home.

All this I learned too late. And meanwhile Mr Rodriguez still wanted the elusive document, tying me and John together. But with the British Consulate doors firmly closed to us, we had no way of getting it.

I was, by this stage, barely eating, and I was beginning to lose a lot of weight. Most days I was having little more than a chapatti and a small portion of channa (chickpeas) or dal (lentils). In my state of distress, the effort of cooking and eating had become too much.

I had been looking for ways to publicise my plight – father trapped in India with two babies – in an effort to get things moving. When I went to see her for some documents, Maria the social worker at Hiranandani Hospital where the girls had been born, had been shocked by my appearance. I had actually been quite beefy when she first met me, but by this time I was skinny. She told me she knew a CNN correspondent and that they might do a news story on my situation. I decided to go on hunger strike, hoping it might help. For the next week I ate nothing and took only water.

In the event CNN did not do the story, and when I went back to see the lawyer Pratik, I told him what I was doing, he shook his head sadly. 'I am sorry you are doing this Andi, but remember that here in India many people go without food – what makes you more special than them?'

He was right. Why did I think refusing food would make a difference to anything? Besides which the nannies, seriously worried about what was going on, had threatened to walk out if I didn't eat. I stopped the hunger strike and began eating again, although I still had very little appetite.

In a last-ditch bid to get things moving, John spoke to Anne-Marie Hutchinson, a lawyer in London who was helping us with a parental order for the girls, making us both equal legal parents to Tara and Amritsar. Anne-Marie was a noted human rights lawyer with a lot of clout. John had got to know her when he applied for the Parental Order, which had to happen within six months of the births. The Parental Order would make us full, equal parents to the girls, as opposed to parent and stepparent, and it would allow the girls to have British birth certificates.

John explained to Anne-Marie the difficulties we were having, and she spoke to the man at the Foreign Office who had so far been no help at all. This time he got his team to speak to the British Consulate in Mumbai and ask them to give us the document we needed.

'Go back there tomorrow,' John said. 'I think they'll help now.'

I was not at all keen to see Daisy or Zubin again, having been unceremoniously packed off and told not to come back. But needs must. The following day I got Ram to drive me to the Consulate.

Inside I asked for Daisy. She was not available. But then Zubin appeared. He, with evident reluctance, led me off to a side room. He then made a note of what we needed, disappeared, and came back with the necessary document. Stuffing it into my bag before he could change his mind, I shot out of the door and into Ram's waiting taxi.

'Success, Mr Andi?' he asked cautiously.

'Success Ram, I have the document. Let's have a celebratory samosa.'

Ram chuckled and head wobbled. 'This is very good news Mr Andi. I think this is possibly a two-samosa moment. From the very best samosa maker in Mumbai. I am very happy, very happy indeed.'

After a detour to visit the 'best samosa maker in Mumbai' a claim validated by a couple of excellent samosas, Ram took me home. 'We're on our way, girls,' I said, picking up first Amritsar and then Tara and dancing round with them, much to Nikki's amusement.

I called John and told him the good news. 'Thank goodness the FO man came through,' he said. 'I was beginning to wonder if those people at the FO actually did anything at all to help stranded British subjects.'

'I'll take the document to the FRRO as soon as I can,' I told him. 'Surely Mr Rodriguez has got to give me the visas now.'

That evening when Manju arrived, I told her the good news.

'This is good Mr Andi,' she said, nodding sagely. 'But as you have had a lot of difficulties getting your visas, you will need to give an extra payment. Do you know what I mean? I think you would need to give 70,000 rupees.'

I looked a bit stunned. She meant a bribe, I understood that. But the sum she mentioned was the equivalent of over £700 and was more than three times the usual 20,000 rupees.

'Are you sure?' I asked her.

Manju nodded firmly. She always seemed to know what was going on. In fact, I was fairly sure there was some kind of network going on between the nannies, the agents and the FRRO.

I duly organised for John to transfer the 70,000 rupees, which I went and cashed. It came in 1000 and 500 rupee bills, so I ended up with a very big wad of cash. How was I going to 'slip' that to the FRRO staff without their security cameras picking it up?

Manju had told me she would let me know when it was the right day to go back to the FRRO. Any day that Mr Rodriguez was not around would have suited me, but I kept quiet, took Manju's advice and on the appointed day Ram and I set off, the cash stuffed into my bag along with the vital document. It was only four days after my last visit to get my own visa extension renewed. By this time, I had visited the FRRO at least 15 times and I was becoming uncomfortably familiar with its bleak corridors and blank-faced officials.

I left Ram outside and went to stand in the queue. When I got to the front, I asked how Tara and Amritsar's visas were progressing. I spoke to a pleasant girl, Praju, who said that their files were all in order. I handed over the final document, the piece of paper that had taken so much time and effort to get. Praju looked at it, then looked up at me and nodded. I took this as a signal. There were security cameras everywhere, so I slipped the wad of notes out of my pocket and into one of the two files that were on my lap.

'The money is there,' I whispered conspiratorially.

Praju's eyes widened in horror. 'No, this is not a good time,' she said, hastily passing back the folders. 'Go outside to the hall and sort this!'

Heart pounding, I grabbed the folder and backed out of the door to the hallway, where I sat on one of the metal benches and tried not to hyperventilate.

I would make a terrible spy, I thought ruefully. I couldn't spot an agent to save my life and now I couldn't even manage to slip Praju a bribe without messing it up.

Sitting in the hall I put my hand into the folder to take the cash out, intending to put it back into my pocket. I looked up – there was a camera at the end of the corridor, but I hoped it was too far away to pick up what I was doing. I wrapped my hand around the stack of notes, pulled them out – and dropped them all over the floor.

It felt like a slow-motion disaster scene as notes flew everywhere. After a brief, horrified moment of paralysis, I fell to my knees and began trying to scoop them up, ignoring the puzzled and curious stares I was attracting. I was so nervous that I grabbed notes and, unable to stack them neatly, scrunched them into a ball in my hand. Except that the ball got too big and notes started falling out of it, so that I was dropping them as fast as I was scooping them up.

Praying that the camera at the end of the hall hadn't recorded this fiasco in full-colour detail, I finally managed to get all the notes into my pocket where they formed a large, awkward-looking bulge. I went back into the office and over to Praju, gave her the folders and said, 'I think I had better go now'.

She nodded, clearly lost for words, and I turned and left.

That evening when Manju arrived, she looked at me, hands on hips.

'Mr Andi, the deal is off.'

'What do you mean?' I tried not to look embarrassed. Had she heard that I'd botched trying to bribe an FRRO official and then made things even worse by scattered wads of cash all over the floor?

'I do not know what happened, but I am hearing that Mr Rodriguez is not happy with you. All he wants is to make you uncomfortable. He wants to see you...what is it when the fish is on the hook?'

'Squirm?'

'Yes,' she nodded vigorously. 'He wants to see you squirm.'

My heart sank.

'So, you're saying there's nothing I can do? I got the document he wanted, and I'm offering money too, and none of that is enough?'

Manju nodded again. 'Yes, that is what I am hearing. Mr Rodriguez does not like it that your Embassy phoned to ask about someone who does not work there.'

I could hardly believe what I was hearing. We were completely trapped – John his end and me mine. No-one was budging, either end, to help us.

On the phone later that day we discussed wild plans to get around the deadlock. It was something we'd been doing with increasing frequency, as the situation became more and more fraught and apparently hopeless.

'One of the people from the Foreign Office told me that your best option might be to head for the Nepalese border and bribe the border guards,' John said. 'Of course, it was unofficial, they'd never admit that they said that. But if that's the best the FO can come up with, maybe we'll have to try it. You could take the train to the border, and I could fly into Kathmandu and get to the border the other side. I'm sure we would be able to get you over.'

'It's a 24-hour journey to the border this side. And even if I could manage that, if I'm caught, I could be accused of child-trafficking,' I said. 'Even though they're my children. I can't risk that. The only way I could do it is if Rehanna came along, since she is down as their mother.'

I took a breath. 'I think I might have to marry her. I know it would be bigamous in the UK, but here our civil partnership is not recognised. I could marry her, and we could probably get the girls out of the country.'

Rehanna had been turning up so frequently that I was giving her around £130 a week in handouts, most recently for her 'sick mama' who now needed a cataract operation. I had been keeping her onside in case we needed her to help us get the girls out and so far, she'd cost us over £2000 (in addition to the surrogacy fees she received from the clinic). Her mother could have had at many dozens of cataract operations and a few spa days too, based on the amount Rehanna was creaming from us.

John was silent for a moment, and then I heard a small sob. 'You can't do that.'

'Oh John, I'm sorry, I don't want to upset you. I'm just so desperate.'

'Not that desperate. You're not doing that. That woman has been milking us dry and I would never trust her to help us. Imagine what she would charge us if we gave her that kind of power. Besides which, I couldn't bear to think of you marrying her, even for show.' He paused. 'I've been thinking that perhaps we could charter a boat and get the girls out that way.'

I was taken aback. I wasn't the only one resorting to wild fantasies.

'Er, where would we go?'

'Well, what about the Maldives?'

'You mean those little islands in the middle of nowhere a few thousand miles away? Are you nuts?'

'Actually, they're only one thousand miles away, a good boat can get there in a couple of days, and from there we could fly home. I know it sounds like a long shot, OK a crazy long shot, but what else are we going to do? I reckon we could give the Harbour Master and the Captain a brown envelope, slip the girls aboard and off we go.'

He was serious. And I had to hand it to him, he had thought of something that just might, failing all else, be possible. But it was fraught with problems, not to mention ridiculously expensive. Chartering a good, sizeable boat plus crew would cost an arm and a leg.

'Well, it beats my other idea,' I told him. 'I was thinking of strapping the girls onto my back and swimming to Saudi.'

We laughed. At least bantering like this about near-impossible ways of escaping from our miserable dilemma cheered us up, if only for a few minutes.

'Let's wait a bit longer,' John said. 'We will get a breakthrough soon, we must.'

'I hope so,' I told him. 'I've got nothing to wear. I sent everything back with Manuela and I've only got four t-shirts and two pairs of trousers.'

I knew that we both tried to stay upbeat, for each other more than for ourselves. And we always tried to say goodnight on a positive note. But I suspected that John's 'we'll get a breakthrough soon' sounded much more confident than either he or I felt.

Diwali, the five-day festival of light was in full flow over the next few days. It marks the Hindu New Year and is a celebration of new beginnings and of good over evil and light over darkness. I hoped it might bring us our own small slice of good fortune.

I stood on our balcony at night, looking out over the car park behind us, where there were many people, men, women and children throwing fireworks. Small children gazed on, fascinated by the coloured lights and the bangs as fireworks exploded. Health and safety were notably absent, as small boys picked up the remnants of still-smouldering fireworks and firecrackers popped along the street as people walked past.

Nikki told me that she and her husband had been selling fireworks in the days leading up to Diwali. Apparently, they made some good money, and after Diwali she went out to buy many plastic rattles and small toys for Tara and Amritsar which was so generous. She also brought us home-make pakoras, potato and chickpea flour fried snacks. I ate one and spent the next 24 hours on the loo regretting it.

I had learned to be incredibly careful about food, although as the pakora story showed, I still made mistakes from time to time. I used to shop every few days at the local Haiko supermarket and I often bought chicken to cook for supper. I've always been a bit paranoid about food hygiene, having trained as a chef, and never more so than around chicken. So, in the supermarket I always asked for polythene bag in order to pick up their packs of pre-packaged chicken portions from the fridge. I didn't know who might have been handling them and how much salmonella there might be hanging around.

One week I turned up to find that a lady in a sari had been assigned to stand beside the chicken cabinet with a pile of plastic bags. She would then open the door of the cabinet and put the chicken into the plastic bags for the customers.

'You see,' the manager said to me. 'We are seeing you ask for the bags to put the chicken and now we are providing assistance.'

'Thank-you,' I said. 'That's very thoughtful.'

In India there was someone for every job, no matter how small. The chicken lady smilingly offered to get my chicken out for me. But I said no, she was picking up the chicken with her hands and goodness knows what else she had touched. I stuck to my own method, although I did appreciate their job-creation initiative.

It was during Diwali that Rehanna arrived again, with a bag of sweets and a smiling request for more urgent funds 'for Mama'. Wearily I handed over yet more cash and ushered her out of the door.

Almost every night I lay awake for hours, listening to the drone of traffic from the main road and wondering what else I could do. I felt close to despair.

Then, tossing and turning through long, hot and noisy night, I made a decision. Early the next morning I got up, packed my few belongings into my rucksack, woke Manju and the girls and told them we were leaving.

'I'm sorry Manju, thank your friend and tell him I will pay the rent I promised, but I can't stay here any longer.'

Manju nodded and after we'd fed the girls, she began packing their belongings while I called Ram, who arrived half an hour later. We piled into the taxi, and I asked Ram to take us to the Marriott's Lakeside Apartments. After many weeks of managing in rundown apartments, I'd had enough, I needed cleanliness and I needed drains that worked.

Chapter 10

<u>Going Home</u>

The staff at the Lakeside remembered us and were very welcoming, but they told me that they didn't take in-person bookings, I could only book an apartment online. I had to go and sit at a computer in the lounge, book an apartment and then go back to reception. After which I was given a key and we moved into a one-bed apartment overlooking the lake.

I called John and told him we'd moved. 'I know it costs more, and I know we can't stay here long,' I said. 'But I need this, just for a while, to try to get my sanity back.'

John was understanding. 'Just take a bit of time and relax,' he said. 'I'm going back to the Indian High Commission with a very big colour photo of the girls and I'm going to demand to know why they are keeping me from my children.'

'Good luck. Give 'em hell,' I said. Not that he hadn't already, I knew that. But another attempt to shame them into giving him what he should have had eight months earlier was worth a try. And what else did we have?

Being back at the Lakeside Apartments was a breath of fresh air – literally. Amazingly, six months after I had last been there, many of the people I had met were still there. My good friends Desi and Sandra were both still there; when they spotted us both of them came rushing up to give me a hug and to marvel over the girls and how they'd grown. I had been so alone in the apartments, where the only other adults were the nannies. Being able to sit in the restaurant and tell them the story of our months in India over a glass of wine felt good.

Manju and Nikki continued to look after the girls, so our routines remained unchanged. The difference was that in the evenings I could go and meet friend's downstairs for a couple of hours, and during the daytime, when I had the girls, I could take them out to the garden area, knowing that here we would be safe.

Within a couple of days Rehanna had tracked us down, with more tales of woe and demands for money. I gave in to the inevitable and paid her. I wasn't going to be able to shake her off until we left India.

While our environment was much better at the Lakeside, I still felt distraught about what had happened to us. It was only a few weeks until Christmas and we were still stranded.

I felt broken by all that had happened, and one evening things came to a head. I was in a state of acute mental distress that was terrifying. I felt strangely dissociated from everything around me and I suddenly knew that I couldn't cope any longer. Terrified that I was having a nervous breakdown all I could think of was to get myself to hospital. I told Manju I had to go out I said I would be back late and then I got in a rickshaw outside the hotel and asked the driver to take me to Hiranandani Hospital.

On the way there I felt as though a dam inside me was about to burst. I knew I had to get to somewhere safe before I let it all out. I paid the driver, walked into Accident and Emergency, and went up to the desk. The receptionist smiled at me, but I couldn't get any words out. Instead, I began crying, sobbing, and shaking and screaming.

I tried to tell them the story and it came out in gulps and sobs, and I just couldn't stop; the dam had burst. 'It's all been too much,' I choked, 'Everyone has taken from us, but no-one will help. Father Gandhi would be disgusted at how his children have treated us. Everywhere there is greed. I can't get home, I can't get my children home, I don't know what else to do.'

Two nurses led me, still sobbing and barely able to stand, into a side room where a doctor came and hooked me up to a heart monitor and stuck an oxygen mask over my face, which had the (probably desired) effect of stopping me in mid-flow.

Later the doctor came back and, after looking at all my test results, sat down on the side of the bed.

'You are having a panic attack,' he said. 'I can hear that you have been having a very difficult time and I am sorry for this. I can give you something to calm you and you need rest. Would you like to stay in the hospital overnight?'

I would have loved to just sink into oblivion, at least for a few hours. But I did not dare take that option. I was afraid that if I stayed, I might be put into a psychiatric hospital and sectioned.

'I'd better not,' I said. 'I have children, I must go back to them. Thank you for your help.'

And so, feeling sick and dazed and clutching a prescription, which I later threw away, I paid my bill and left the hospital, breakdown over. The whole episode had been frightening and traumatic, worse than anything else I'd experienced since I arrived in India. But I knew that somehow, I would have to cope. The girls were my priority, and no matter how terrible I felt, I wasn't going to let them down. I had needed an outlet, and I'd found one.

I went home and called John. I told him what had happened.

'I'm worried about you,' he said. 'I'd do anything to be there. You're an incredibly strong person, you can get through this, I know you can.'

'I will,' I said. 'I know I will.'

It was very late by the time I sank into bed, exhausted, and wrung out. I could not even think about what the next steps would be.

And then, the following day, John called again.

'Andi, they said my visa is going to be granted. I'm getting it. I will be with you in a few days.'

I needed him to repeat the news, so that I could take it in. All I could think was, 'Our nightmare is over. Thank-you, whatever gods or forces or powers are out there, thank-you'.

A few days later Ram drove us to the airport to meet John.

'This is very cheerful news Mr Andi,' he said, his head wobbling so hard I worried about how he was managing to drive. 'You are finding fortune again, after a most difficult time, and I am very happy for you.'

'Thank-you Ram, I will miss you when I leave. You have helped me a great deal.'

Ram grinned broadly. 'It is not every day that I find such a nice customer as you Mr Andi. One who likes conversation and appreciates a samosa to break the journey from time to time. This is a very special customer.'

I felt honoured. And it was good to feel that there were some things, and some people, that I would miss when I left India. Ram was one of the good guys.

The arrivals area in Mumbai airport is outside. After immigration you go down a long corridor before exiting onto an open square, flanked by railings and seating. This was where we waited, in the hot midday sun. We stood to one side, close to a small hut that housed a taxi company, trying to find a bit of shade. I stood with Manju and Nikki on either side, each holding one of the girls. John and I had never imagined that we would be apart for eight long months. Now I longed to see him with an intensity that felt overwhelming. Would he have changed? Had I?

Would we be able to go home and pick up the pieces of our life together after all that we'd been through?

'Andi!'

I turned to see him coming out of the entrance to the terminal, waving at me. I waved back, furiously, and moments later we were in each other's arms. A hug so warm and heartfelt that it spoke a thousand words.

Laughing and tearful, I held a handout either side of me. 'Here are your daughters.'

John stood looking from Amritsar to Tara and back again, speechless. Nikki and Manju smiled, while the girls stared at John with big eyes.

'This is your Daddy, Tara, Amritsar. Daddy is here at last.'

John looked from one small face to the other. He was careful not to startle them. They had to get to know him, we both knew that. It would take time.

'Manju, Nikki, this is John.'

'Welcome Mr John,' Manju said. 'We are happy that you are here. Mr Andi is very, very happy.'

She was right, I was. I kept my eyes on him as if he might disappear in a puff of smoke if I looked away. I had dreamed of this day for eight long months.

Ram was hovering behind us, grinning broadly. I introduced him and he held out his hand. 'Mr John we are honoured to have you here in India. Please come this way to my car. Let me help you with your bag.'

We made our way to the car, where we all squeezed in. It wasn't until we were seated in the taxi that a few tears slid down John's cheeks as he sat between Tara and Amritsar, holding one small hand in each of his.

Ram drove us across the hot, bustling city to the Lakeside Apartments. It reminded me of the first time John, and I had arrived, full of hope and dreams, just over two years earlier. Then we had been almost overwhelmed by the scent of India, that heady mix of spice, bodies, animals, and traffic fumes. Now I was so used to it I barely noticed any more.

Once John had dropped his things off in our room, we left the nannies settling the girls for their nap and went down to the restaurant to get something to eat. Over lunch we made plans to go to the FRRO the following day and then to get home, as soon as possible.

'You look skinny,' John told me.

'That's not the only way in which I've changed,' I said. 'This has all taken such a toll. I feel angry, hurt and disillusioned.'

'I'm not surprised,' John said. 'It's been harder than we ever imagined, and I've been worried about you. I'm so sorry that you've had to go through such a tough time.'

'You have too,' I said. 'I know I sometimes envied you, being the one at home, but I know it was awful for you, unable to be with us.' For John it had been a long, lonely vigil. He had kept himself busy with work, the dogs, and the house, but he had missed out on his children's first eight months, and he had lived with the constant stress and worry, just as I had. And, not wanting to worry others, he had not talked to anyone about what was happening.

'I have nightmares about Mr Rodriguez,' I said. I was only half-joking. 'You'll meet him yourself tomorrow.'

I can't wait,' John replied dryly.

Ram drove us – me, John, the nannies, and the girls – to the FRRO for what I hoped, with every fibre of my being, was the last time.

'It's like something out of a Hemingway novel,' John remarked, as he took in the slow-turning ceiling fans and the flies, the lino floors, and the elderly desks.

After we had queued for an hour Mr Rodriguez appeared. Carrying an armful of heavy files, he sat at a desk and, ignoring John completely, spoke to me.

'Well Mr Webb, here you are again,' he said with what I could have sworn was a smirk.

'Yes, Mr Rodriguez, and this is John, my partner and the girls' biological father.'

He appeared to notice John for the first time.

'Ah, so you are the babies' father,' he said. 'Here at last.'

'We are both the fathers,' John said firmly. 'The paperwork makes that clear.'

Faced with the prospect of finally having to grant Tara and Amritsar's exit visas, Mr Rodriguez did his best to wring every last ounce of misery from the situation. He turned back to me.

'I'm afraid that you must pay a fine, Mr Webb, as you have overstayed your visa,' he said, looking at me like a head teacher with a disobedient schoolboy. There is a daily fine for this. '

'That is, as you know Mr Rodriguez, because I could not leave, since my daughters were unable to leave.'

'Nonetheless, you must pay before your own exit visa can be granted. The babies also have a fine, they have British passports but no visa so they must pay a fine for every day they have stayed here since their passports were issued.'

'But...they had no visa because you wouldn't give them one. And they were born here!'

'These are the rules,' Mr Rodriguez said, his face set like stone.

We paid. After which he told us to go away for half an hour and come back to collect the passports. We did, and to our huge relief, all three passports had been stamped with the exit visas.

As we turned to go, Mr Rodriguez beckoned me over to him. Smiling paternally, he said, 'I hope you know Mr Webb; this was not personal.' He laughed loudly. 'I am happy to see you smiling now. Last week you were in tears, you have had a very bad time of things here. I doubt you will return to India again, will you?'

'I don't know, Mr Rodriguez. We might come back to India; it is a beautiful country. But I hope very much that we will never, ever need to come back to this office.'

For a second, he looked taken aback. Then he laughed again. 'Good luck with your children and your life in the UK,' he said. 'Yours are the last British surrogate babies born to a same sex couple to leave India, by the way.' He turned and disappeared through his office door. It was the first time; in all the weeks I had been going to his office that he had referred to the girls as my children.

'Let's go,' I hissed to John, and we headed out to Ram's taxi and back to Lakeside, where we celebrated by booking our tickets home for three days' time and then taking the girls out to the pool for a play. They were already at ease with John, it was as if they knew he was theirs, just as I was, and as we each bobbed one of the girls around in the shallow end they squealed with joy.

'I hadn't realised we were the last gay couple to leave India with surrogate babies,' John said.

'Me neither,' I replied. 'Though I have been kept here for a very long time.'

The law had changed and from then on only heterosexual couples married for a minimum of two years would be allowed to use surrogacy.

We were both silent for a moment, aware of just how close we had been to disaster and just how far we had come.

I hoped we had left Rehanna behind when we moved to Lakeside, so her appearance at our door the next day startled me. She had brought her brother and her two children. In they all came, Rehanna declaring how happy she was to meet John and how lovely the girls were. Then she announced that she had a bank account and would like John to make regular payments to her.'

'I am twins' mother,' she declared. 'My children,' she nudged them forward, 'twins' brother and sister.'

She handed John a piece of paper with her bank details on it. He took it and put it on the table.

'You are not our children's mother,' he said. 'You were our surrogate. That is not the same thing.'

'I am mama,' she said, raising her voice. 'You pay me. Money for Mama.'

Her 'money for Mama' which had initially been about her own mother, now clearly referred to herself. She was the 'Mama' as far as she was concerned, and we owed her.

John turned away and I could see he was struggling to contain his anger. I stepped forward.

'Rehanna it is time to go now. John is tired from his flight.'

I ushered her towards the door and her brother and children followed. She was still muttering, 'I am mama'. I handed her 10,000 rupees, just over £100, pushed her gently out of the door and then shut it. I turned and leaned against it, looking over at John. He picked up the piece of paper with her bank details, screw it up and threw it in the bin.

'I never want to hear another word about that dratted woman again, he said. 'Her behaviour is insulting.'

'We did need to keep her onside,' I reminded him.

'I know,' he said. 'But not anymore. We paid her for her nine months service, and we've paid her all over again. Now it stops.'

I breathed a sigh of relief. Perhaps I should have told her to go away the first time she showed up. But I was concerned that she could make trouble for us in getting the girls out of India and that we might need her help.

What the story did illustrate, all too painfully, is why it's rarely a good idea to have contact with a surrogate. It was the British Embassy that insisted we meet in the first place, and they, inadvertently, had put me in a difficult situation.

Saying goodbye to my friends at Lakeside, to the nannies, to Ram and to India itself over the following couple of days seemed almost unreal. I had dreamed of this moment for so long, but there was sadness too. India, with all its beauty, poverty, generosity, and corruption, had been my home for eight months. It had given us our children and it would forever be a part of them, and of us.

Eighteen Moons

At the airport Ram pumped my hand up and down. 'I am missing you Mr Andi. Do not think badly of India. Come back again.'

'I will miss you too Ram,' I said. 'India is full of good people, and you are one of them. I hope I will see you again one day.'

He grinned. 'Of course. We will go for a samosa. Yes?'

'Yes.' I laughed.

As I walked into the terminal, holding Amritsar in one arm and my bag in the other, I turned for one last look at India. Ram stood beside his car, waving to us. Behind him the heat of another Mumbai day shimmered over the city. I waved, and turned back to follow John and Tara to check in.

Queuing to go through passport control, I began to feel anxious. It was entirely possible that something could go wrong at this late stage, and they could stop us. We got to the front of the queue and the official looked at our passports.

'Where is the paperwork relating to the surrogacy?' he asked.

My heart sank. I had packed it and our cases had been checked in. I groaned. 'I don't have it,' I explained. 'It is in my suitcase. I thought the passports and the visas would be enough.'

He tipped his head back and looked at me, as if appraising me. Beside me I could feel John's tension.

The official appeared to come to a decision. He smiled. 'The passports are enough. You can go through'.

I could have wept.

Half an hour later we were on board our British Airways flight. But it was only once we had taken off that we were able to relax. John and I looked at one another.

'We made it,' I said.

The cabin staff made a fuss of the girls and offered to hold them for us while we ate. The flight was over nine hours, and when Tara and Amritsar were sleeping between feeds I tried to doze and thought about what it would be like to be home.

Would I find it easy to adjust? I wasn't sure. Would I have the equivalent of Stockholm Syndrome, in which those who have been kidnapped fall in love with their kidnappers? Would I find that India, for all the heartache she had put me through, meant more to me now than England? Well, I would find out.

And then there was Manuela, who was still living in our London flat, waiting to take over as nanny to the girls. I wasn't sure how I felt about her, after all that had happened in India.

She had left me high and dry. But John had employed her, and I had agreed that it was simpler to keep her on than to find someone new at short notice.

As we touched down, I began to feel excited. But the cold and dark of a grey November day was a shock. It was just four weeks to Christmas, so lights and decorations were everywhere, their garish colours bright in the gloom.

A taxi journey later and we were back at the flat. By the time we got in the girls, and I were shivering – none of us had enough clothes on, although we'd wrapped the girls in blankets. Their small faces peered around them, no doubt wondering what this strange, cold place was. 'We're here girls,' I told them. 'This is home.'

Chapter 11

Fresh Hope in Thailand

How happy I was to see Remus and Gracie, our crazy, rapscallion hounds. And how happy they were to see me! One of the many wonderful things about dogs is they never forget you, and they don't hold back when it comes to showing you just how much you are loved. They leapt on me, tails going like pistons, drooling with delight, licking, and nuzzling for all they were worth. I loved it. I'd missed them so much.

Over the next few days, I gradually adjusted to being home. I was filled with gratitude every day, waking up in our own flat, giving the girls breakfast as John got ready for work, and then spending time each day getting used, bit by bit, to life as it was. I went shopping for groceries, cooked meals I hadn't had for eight months (oh the bliss of a simple Shepherd's Pie) and dug out my winter clothes.

Should I have seen a counsellor to help me come to terms with the anguish of the final few months in India? It had been a grim ordeal, so probably. But I didn't. With the girls to look after, not to mention the dogs, I was busy and that in itself was therapeutic.

Our friends and family were delighted that we were home. Kayla sent me a message saying she and Jamie were thrilled. My mother, such a generous support to me during all those months, couldn't wait to plan a visit to the UK to meet her grandchildren. John's family in Ireland were the same, longing to welcome Tara and Amritsar to the family.

Manuela had been waiting when we arrived. She'd had little to do in the weeks we were still in India, other than look after the dogs. Now she was back on nanny duty, and it was a squeeze with the five of us in the flat. She had the second bedroom, and the girls were in the tiny box room.

Being with Manuela had already started to grate. She took the girls out for long 'walks' in their pushchair, during which they slept, and she probably sat in a cafe reading a magazine and sipping a coffee. When she brought them back, they were wide awake and raring to go, just as Manuela clocked off for the day, leaving me to tire them out before bedtime. So, when we went down to Long River at the weekend, I was grateful that we left Manuela behind with the flat to herself.

I couldn't wait to be in the house that was truly home, where it would be just the four of us – and the dogs – for a whole weekend. As we stepped through the large, oak door, John looked at me expectantly. I laughed. 'OK, I know how hard you've been working; I'm ready to be amazed'.

And I was. I walked from room to room, admiring the paintwork, the colours, the finishes, and the furnishings. He had worked hard, and I was duly wowed.

Christmas was only three weeks away and I threw myself into preparations. We had so much to celebrate; our first Christmas with our girls and I was determined to do it in style. I insisted John help me lug home a huge tree, and then spent a whole afternoon decorating it with all the baubles and glitter I could find. After that it was out to the woods to find foliage, holly, and armfuls of greenery. By the time I'd finished the house looked like an enchanted forest, with holly winding up the old oak staircase and the gilt picture frames all draped with every kind of seasonal greenery. As we worked – a bemused John was roped in to help – we played carols. And by the time we'd finished the house looked impressive.

The weekend was a time when John could be with the girls full-time and he threw himself into feeding, winding, changing, and sleeping routines. I didn't want to keep saying, 'this is how you do it' and I soon realised I didn't need to; John took to it all easily and was clearly loving it. We didn't disagree over much, but when it came to swaddling, he wasn't keen. I had got into the habit of it, because all the Indian nannies did it, but I agreed that the girls didn't need it any longer.

I was sad when it was time to go back to London, the weekend, with the peace of the country and time for the four of us together, had been wonderful.

Manuela was not endearing herself to either me or John. As he changed Amritsar's nappy, she snapped at him, 'that's not how you do it, let me show you'. Seeing the expression of disbelief on his face she thought better of it and said, 'or perhaps you could google it'. John had kept Manuela on for months, even though she'd had almost nothing. He didn't deserve a put-down like that. He said very little, but that was the moment when she lost his confidence and support. She had ten days off over Christmas and New Year, which gave us a welcome period of time to ourselves.

We had a wonderful holiday week at Long River. Family and friends were invited, the girls were showered with presents and passed from one adoring pair or hands to another, and the crisp chill of the English countryside was at its best. I began to relax. I was home, and all was well.

After the festivities we had a quiet few days and began to look forward to the New Year. I still hadn't given up hope of another pregnancy in Thailand and in late December, Nancy, the administrator at the All-IVF Clinic told me that the surrogate had agreed to have another try and everything was looking good.

This small flame of hope still felt very important to me. But at the same time, as John and I toasted 2014, I thought about all that the past year had brought. It had been extraordinary, sometimes wonderful sometimes terrifying. But here I was, with a loyal and kind partner in life, two beautiful daughters, two crazy dogs and a lovely home. Whatever came next, I told myself, I was a lucky man.

In early January Manuela returned. And while we needed the help, I found being around her hard. I still felt very let down by her, after she bolted from India, leaving me alone with two babies. And her defection aside, her manner had not improved a bit. If anything, she was more opinionated and demanding than ever.

I didn't even feel she was much help. She was still taking the girls out all afternoon and bringing them back at 5pm, both of them, having slept all afternoon, completely hyper and impossible to calm in time for bed. I put up with her because John had hired her, and he thought we needed her. But just two weeks into the New Year, on his birthday, they had an argument.

Manuela was in the habit of leaving the double buggy downstairs in the narrow front hallway of our block of flats, instead of bringing it up to the flat in the lift. Inevitably John or I would have to go down and get it. So, when she did it yet again John asked her, firmly but politely to go and bring the buggy upstairs. Manuela refused, insisting that she couldn't do it and shouldn't have to.

Coming soon after the 'you could google it' episode, this pushed John to break point.

'Enough is enough,' he told me. 'She has to go'. I was in full agreement. Manuela was not the person we needed to help us make this big adjustment as a family. Days later she left, sullenly dragging her bag out of the flat without bothering to say goodbye. And just like that, a cloud was lifted from over us. I had been feeling as though I could barely breathe with her around, but the day she left I started smiling again.

A day or two after Manuela left the new Russian neighbour, Natalia, came in to say hello. She seemed very keen to come in and see the children. Was she checking up on us? I knew Manuela had talked to her. What had she said? I invited Natalia in and introduced her to Tara and Amritsar, both in their highchairs in the kitchen, where I was feeding them mashed banana. Conscious that I was being scrutinised I hovered a spoon of banana slop over Tara – and it fell straight into her eye. As I leapt for a flannel Tara bawled and my heart sank, fearing that Natalia was probably about to go and report us to social services.

Thankfully that didn't happen. Natalia laughed and she soon became a good friend. And confided that Manuela had indeed been hinting that we were not adequate parents. I could only thank heaven that she had gone.

We decided after that to do without a nanny, at least for a few weeks, while we all settled down to life together. I got the girls into a good routine and John did his bit in the early mornings and nights. Over the weekends at Long River, he revelled in being a dad, playing with the girls, bathing them, and putting them to bed. It was clear to me, even then, that he was going to be the soft touch parent who always broke the rules, while I was going to have to be the tough one who said no. I didn't always relish this role, but what I loved most was that we were parenting the girls together. Every time I watched John running around with a giggly small girl on his shoulders, the nightmare aspects of my time in India slipped a little further into the past.

Kayla, who had become such a good companion in India, had become a firm friend. She and Jamie lived in the north of England, so we didn't get to meet up often, but when we did it was enormous fun. Sometimes she and I met up in London, without the children, for a catch up over a glass of wine, and other times we met with all four children and partners, and Kayla's mum and dad sometimes came too. When we all got together, six adults and four children, Kayla and I always ended up laughing about the fertility temple trip and my revered status as father of four.

If only, I thought ironically. Being a father was everything I wanted. So when, in mid-January, I got an email from Nancy at the All-IVF Clinic saying that the pregnancy had been confirmed, I was over the moon.

'Don't get too excited,' John warned. 'Wait until its a few months along before you celebrate.' He was right, of course. So far three surrogate pregnancies had ended for me, two in India and one in Thailand. I had no reason, other than blind optimism, to assume that this one would work out.

Life as a full-time dad of two kept me busy. The girls were awake at dawn and, apart from nap time in the middle of the day, full-on straight through until bedtime at 6.30pm. Both were crawling – at full-tilt all too often – and were pulling themselves up on the furniture and grabbing at every interesting looking object in sight. Cue time to remove all low-level ornaments and potentially dangerous items from both homes.

By bedtime each evening – their bedtime that is – I was exhausted and barely up to cooking dinner for me and John, let alone any kind of meaningful conversation.

'I think perhaps we should think about getting another nanny,' he said one evening, as he regarded my exhausted body, slumped on the sofa.

'I think perhaps you're right,' I agreed sleepily. 'But this time we choose together.'

We advertised for a live-in au pair, working 30 hours a week, rather than the standard 20, but for a more generous living wage. We had almost 700 applicants. This was a time when, after the major recession of 2008, half of Europe wanted to come to the UK for a better life. We had applications from both male and female Spanish students, Italian office workers, German engineers, and French ski instructors. We even had an application from a German Abercrombie and Fitch Model! It was with some difficulty, but we narrowed it down to three interviews. And in the end, we picked 20-year-old Essie, an English girl from Tunbridge Wells in Kent.

She was like a breath of fresh air, bright and full of cheerful enthusiasm. Her father was in the armed forces, so her parents had mostly lived abroad, and she'd spent a lot of time in posh boarding schools. Interestingly her grandmother had been the head of the Women's Institute in 2000 when members of a small local WI in Yorkshire got together to make a cheeky calendar, posing in very discreet naked shots to raise money for leukaemia research. They caused a ripple so big that it led to a film and thousands of imitators. Essie's granny had been the one who decided it was a 'local matter' when it was referred to the WI leaders for permission, and she had allowed them to go ahead.

Essie wanted to au pair as a sort of internship, she said (I wasn't sure what she thought it would lead to, but fine) so we knew she wouldn't stay for more than a few months. But she seemed like what we needed at that moment. She started work just after my birthday in February and from the start we liked having her around. Helpful, good-natured, and willing to learn, she absolutely adored the girls, and for that we loved her.

In late February came the news that I most dreaded. The pregnancy in Thailand had ended. I felt desperately sad. Why did this keep happening? Every time I mourned for the life that had begun and been so brief. What was it that kept going wrong? Was I destined never to father a child? Surely fate could not be so cruel.

I wondered whether it was time to call it quits. Accept that I would never father a child and concentrate on the children we had together. But I wasn't ready to give up. I needed another roll of the dice. I asked the clinic if another surrogate could be found, for a fresh try. A week later they said they had found someone suitable, a young woman named Ausa who was unmarried (as in India, she needed to be, otherwise her husband would have been deemed the baby's father by the British authorities). I gave the go-ahead and could do no more than hope against hope that this time I might be lucky.

In March it was the girls' first birthday. We held their party in our London flat, with friends and neighbours coming to help celebrate. It was a day filled with presents and laughter, a day of pure joy, when we could put all the heartache of the past year behind us and just be happy. Tara and Amritsar took it all in their stride, crawling around amidst the wrapping paper, mouths pink with cake and icing.

A day earlier I had phoned Kayla. Millie and Max had been born the day before our girls. 'Happy Birthday guys' I yelled down the phone. 'They can't hear you Andi,' Kayla laughed. They were having their own big celebration and she was in a great mood.

It was only a few days after the birthday party that I heard from Nancy in Thailand. Another implantation had taken place – on the girls' birthday. It had to be a lucky omen. I felt from the start that it was different this time.

The next email, a couple of weeks later, told me that the pregnancy hormone had been detected. Followed, four weeks later, by one to say that the heartbeat had been detected. Ausa was carrying my child. Once again John urged caution, and I did try, but I couldn't help feeling, deep down, that this child was going to make it.

Both Tara and Amritsar were close to walking. Tara had, for some time, been able to stand just holding onto my thumbs, so I was sure she would walk first. She loved playing 'steps' — lurching along as I gently led her. Amritsar hadn't been as interested at first, but she began to catch up, hauling herself to her feet on the furniture and looking incredibly pleased with herself as she wobbled back and forth, trying to stay upright. In the end it was Amritsar who walked first, at 14 months, in late May. Tara followed two months later, in July. Once they were on their feet there was no stopping them. We needed eyes in the backs of our heads to manage them, as one would stagger towards the kitchen while the other headed for the French windows, both of them full of baby chuckles at the delight of being mobile. They kept all three of us, me, John, and Essie, busy running around after them.

Sadly, Essie had to move on, so we were on the hunt for a new au pair. Through an au pair website, we found Carla, a 19-year-old Slovenian girl who seemed warm, competent, and friendly. We knew she would need to cover for me while I was in Thailand, a few months down the line. I would be going in December, if all went to plan, and might be away for a couple of months. It would mean taking sole responsibility for the girls while John was at work and working much longer hours, but she said she was very willing to do this.

The updates on Ausa's pregnancy kept coming and the news was good. Emails arrived with photos of the monthly scans, showing a single baby, and I pored over them, absorbing every tiny detail of this minute person who was going to come into our lives. By the start of August, the baby was into its tenth week, and we were beginning to make plans. Thailand, it seemed was better organised and far easier to navigate than India. So, despite all the problems we'd had getting the girls home, I was optimistic and expected Thailand to be a piece of cake by comparison. And then disaster struck. On August 11 a story was published about a twin surrogate birth in Thailand. The girl was fully healthy, but the boy had Down Syndrome and the Australian parents didn't want him.

Baby Gammy, as he became known, was very soon world-famous. He and his sister Pipah had been born in December 2013, but the story only came to light months later. The biological parents had gone back to Australia with Pipah, leaving Gammy with his surrogate mum, Pattaramon, who had decided to raise him herself.

In the aftermath of this story a huge sum of money was raised internationally to help baby Gammy. And all kinds of other unsavoury surrogacy stories came to light. One was about a wealthy Japanese man, Mitsutoki Shigeta who had fathered 13 babies through surrogacy in Thailand. Three he had taken home, but nine others, with nine nannies and a pregnant surrogate were found in a Bangkok apartment. To our horror the clinic responsible was the one we were using, the All IVF Clinic, where the doctor in charge, Dr Pisit Tantiwattanakul , was the man who had orchestrated our embryo creation and pregnancy.

The final outcome of these stories did not happen until two or three years later. It was found that the Australian parents had in fact wanted baby Gammy, but the surrogate mother had decided to keep him. By the time this emerged both babies had settled with their families, so the court ruled that Gammy should stay in Thailand and Pipah in Australia. Both loved, but unable to be raised together.

Mr Shigeta was also allowed to keep all his children. The court ruled that, far from 'baby farming' as had been suspected, he simply wanted a big family, and he could afford to raise them in comfort, so off they all went to Japan.

However, in the summer of 2014 all anyone knew was the lurid headlines, and the Thai military government did not like this one bit. They ruled that paid surrogacy was illegal and a criminal offence, all the surrogacy clinics were apparently shut down and surrogate babies were prevented from leaving the country with their parents, leaving hundreds of families stranded.

Watching all this, John and I were horrified. The clinic we used was shut down and we had no idea where this left us – or our baby. We tried to contact the clinic, but there was no response, our emails were bounced back. The silence of the days that followed was soul-destroying. Where was our surrogate, and our baby? Would we ever even get to see him or her? I couldn't believe that, now a baby was on the way, I might be deprived of holding my child in my arms.

Then, after four long and painful weeks, an email arrived from Natmanee, the nurse at the clinic, saying that the staff were still there and that our surrogate was fine. However, everyone was unsure of what the mood and the legal situation in Thailand was. All Natmanee could say was that all would be well. And all I could do was trust that she was right.

Chapter 12

<u>New Life in Nepal</u>

Hugely relieved to know that the clinic was, in some form at least, still open, I could only hope and pray that all would be well with Ausa and our child and that I would be able to be with our son for his birth in December.

Every week I emailed Nancy, the receptionist at the clinic, to ask how things were. I received very brief replies, never more than a line or two. Her English was not good, so the brevity was probably due to this, rather than anything else, but it was hard to feel reassured when we received such scant information. She did send scans, every now and then and this, more than anything, kept us hopeful that all was on track.

It was one of these scans that showed us, quite clearly, that our baby was a boy. While we never minded what sex our children were, it was good to think that our girls would now have a brother. We couldn't have been happier.

Before the scandal erupted, I had planned to request a fresh attempt at pregnancy. Not only was I still fearful that something might go wrong, I was also keen to have one more child. John and I had agreed that four children, two fathered by each of us, would be perfect. We hoped, all being well, that we might have our last child a year or so down the line.

I knew that the embryos produced after the first egg donation would be, as they always are, graded. The grades range from 1 to 4 and I knew that the very best ones would have been used for the first two pregnancy attempts and the current pregnancy. There were six left, but I knew that they were of poorer quality. I decided the best thing would be to ask for Rene to make a second egg donation, so that there could be new embryos prepared and we could then use the best.

I contacted Sophie at the agency in South Africa and she was warm and encouraging. She said that although things appeared to be shutting down in Thailand the clinic, as we knew, had not exactly ceased operating. And since the law being brought in was against surrogacy, not embryo production – as far as we knew – there was nothing to prevent Rene – who knew the clinic as she'd been there before – returning to the clinic for a further egg donation. This would be her final one, Sophie told me, and she would combine the trip with a visit to her Australian boyfriend on the way home. Sophie said she would organise the trip as soon as possible.

A week later Rene flew to Thailand. Sophie was in touch with me all the way through and she told me that Rene had said all went well, although the clinic was far quieter than on previous occasions. The international clientele had disappeared, and with them the buzz of the place. Now there were just a few Thai couples there. But Dr Pisit was cheerful and so was his nurse, Natmanee and the administrator, Nancy. The clinic had been raided by the police, but all the vital paperwork and the cryo storage facilities had been safely removed to the hotel above the clinic. Rene reported that the egg retrieval went ahead with no problems. She discovered later that she was the very last egg donor to visit the clinic. Soon after that Nancy told me that I now had a fresh set of 12 embryos, safely stored at the clinic.

The only question was what to do with them. As the lurid international headlines continued and the legal net closed around the Thai surrogacy network, it looked unlikely that we would be able to have another surrogate in Thailand. An email from the clinic confirmed this – we would either have to have the embryos destroyed, keep them in Thailand, with no prospect of them being used, or ship them out as soon as possible. Sophie told me that, although she had recently stopped working with Tammuz, the Israeli surrogacy agency its boss, Doron, was the man for me to contact. He would be able to get the embryos transported to a new, safer destination – Nepal.

I hadn't spoken to Doron since we'd met the previous May in India at Lakeside. But he remembered me immediately and said he could help. He had connections which would allow him to transport the embryos over to the Grande City Clinic in Kathmandu and to then arrange for a surrogate. This clinic was the only one, at that time, that would accept embryos without the full documentation. Nepal was not a forward or modern country, it was still languishing behind so many others, and in this situation, it was to our advantage.

Nepal had become the new surrogacy hotspot for same-sex and unmarried couples. We were not the only ones looking for a new safe destination for our embryos and a new surrogate; many other couples were choosing this option.

Delighted and relieved that our embryos would be saved, we signed a surrogacy agreement and paid the shipping fees. It took some time, but at the end of October eight of the new embryos were shipped to Nepal. It was just in time – the clinic in Thailand was completely shut down and Dr Pisit disappeared for several weeks. He did eventually reappear and give himself up to the Thai authorities. Despite all the bluster in the press he was never charged and a couple of years later he opened an IVF clinic in Laos.

We now had eight embryos in a clinic in Nepal, and a baby due to be born – illegally – in Thailand at Christmas.

Doron asked us whether we would like to attempt a pregnancy straight away in Nepal. Given my record so far, we imagined that a first and perhaps a second attempt might well get nowhere. It could well be months or a year down the line before a successful pregnancy was created – if it ever was. I was still very wary, believing the Thai pregnancy to be a one-off and fearful that something could go wrong even at this late stage. We told Doron to go ahead.

Did we have doubts? I did not, but John was perhaps more uncertain. I was thinking that I might never have a chance for another child without the Nepal option, whereas John was thinking, well we already have two children and another on the way – isn't that enough. However, he understood how much it meant to me to keep the possibility of more children alive and so he put his own doubts to one side and was generous in supporting me. There was also, of course, the financial consideration. Finding the money for the surrogacies we'd had so far had taken hard work and sacrifice and at each new step we had to consider carefully whether we could afford it. The whole Indian venture had already well exceeded our planned budget. But while finances could not be ignored, we also felt that you can't put a price on having children. For us to have the family we longed for, we were prepared to dig deep and make economies in other areas.

Our surrogate in Nepal was once again to be Indian. Tammuz used an agency in Delhi to supply surrogates, who would then travel to Nepal and, if the implantation was successful, remain there for the whole nine months, give birth and then return home having been away 'working' for a year or so. A surrogate for us was already in Nepal, so there would be no delay in implantation.

Just over a week later we received news that the pregnancy hormone had been detected at the eight-day stage. We were both shell-shocked; it wasn't what we had expected. I had been so certain that the first attempt wouldn't work. But it seemed that our surrogate, Sushila, was pregnant. Would it become viable? It seemed that it would – at six weeks the heartbeat was detected.

I was busy making plans to travel to Thailand for the birth of our son. We were told that he would be born by caesarean section on December 22. I began to believe that it was actually going to happen – we were having another child, a boy, and this time I was going to be a genetic parent.

We explained to Carla that she would need to give John a lot of support – working long hours as a full-time nanny – while I was away. And although we hoped that would not be for more than a few weeks we couldn't be sure that it wouldn't be longer.

I felt optimistic, I was sure we could wrap the whole thing up in six weeks, but John thought I was being wildly optimistic and that we should prepare for at least three months. Luckily Carla was fine with it, which was a relief for John, who this time would have not only two dogs and a company to take care of in my absence, but two small girls as well.

I hated the thought of leaving Tara and Amritsar. We had been together since the day they were born, and I couldn't imagine being without them for a week, never mind a couple of months. But there was no other option. They had to stay, and I had to be the one to go. This would be John's time with them as their only parent.

A few days before I left, we received astonishing news. In Kathmandu not only was the pregnancy progressing well but we were going to have twins again and they were due in July the following year, less than six months after our son. This was extraordinary news and not something either of us had imagined. We hadn't expected a successful pregnancy this soon, and we certainly hadn't expected twins. We had pictured four children, perhaps, but never five.

In India several embryos had been implanted, so we were not hugely surprised that we had twins. But in Thailand and in Nepal only two embryos were implanted each time. In Thor's case, one had taken and that was, at most, what we hoped for in Nepal. Can you imagine, to hear that both embryos had taken was extraordinary.

The thought of becoming a family of seven left us stunned and by turns excited and terrified. John began thinking about cars that would fit them all, I realised that I might barely be home from Thailand when I would need to leave again for Nepal. We both walked around with slightly dazed expressions for the next few days, having slightly disjointed conversations with ourselves and one another.

'We're going to have five children under the age of three.'

'We'll need five of everything.'

'We don't have enough bedrooms.'

'We certainly can't keep five children in the London flat.'

'We're not going to get any sleep for the next few years...if ever.'

'Imagine five teenagers, all rebelling at once.'

'We'll have to find the right schools for all of them.'

'OK, don't even go there. Let's just stick with trying to imagine five toddlers.'

'The chaos, the feeding, the clothes and nappies and...'

'The joy.' We both reached that conclusion, every day, before going around the whole loop again. It took time for the news to sink in. There were moments of sheer panic, in which one or other of us came close to hyperventilating at the thought of all that would be involved.

But for me, despite all the potential complications, there was something absolutely wonderful and magical about the news. I had felt very bleak about the pregnancies that had ended. As though somehow there was something wrong with me. If I had been religious, I might have felt that God was sending me tests of my endurance. Now, suddenly, after so much heartache I was to be the biological father of three of our children.

I still hadn't fully digested the news when I kissed John, the girls and the dog's goodbye and left for Thailand. It was only a few days before Christmas, and I wouldn't be with them. Remembering the wonderful Christmas, we'd had the previous year, when we all got home from India, I felt sad. The decorations were up, and I'd wrapped the girls' presents before I left. But I wouldn't be there to see them opened.

During the 13-hour flight I felt alone and apprehensive. What lay ahead of me? Would Thailand prove to be as difficult as India? Had I been crazily naive to have another child abroad, after that experience?

I arrived in Bangkok's hugely busy Suvarnabhumi Airport and got a taxi to the Langsuan Executive Apartments which were an hour away in the Sukhumvit Road area. This is one of the city's most buzzing areas, with plenty of high-rise buildings, bars, clubs, hotels, and shopping centres. The Sukhumvit Road is one of the longest in the world, running almost to the Cambodian border. The section in Bangkok is bursting with people and heavy with traffic 24 hours a day, it's hard to believe that until World War Two this was an area of paddy fields.

The Langsuan apartments were part of the Marriot chain – yes, echoes of Mumbai again. I had a small apartment with a living room, an ensuite bedroom and a kitchenette. That night I phoned home, to talk to John and to say hello to Amritsar and Tara, both of whom, John said, looked puzzled to hear Dadda but not see him. I missed them so much already.

The next morning, I went to visit the new premises of Dr Pisit's clinic. In marked contrast to the simple surroundings of the clinic I had visited the previous year to make my deposit, the clinic had now taken over an entire floor of the Athenee Tower, a very plush office block with uniformed doormen and marble everywhere. It seemed that the bad publicity had simply sent the clinic up in the world.

Inside I met Nancy, the administrator who I had met the previous time. She introduced me to Joy, who she told me would assist me with all the paperwork. Joy was friendly and helpful, she spoke good English and she told me she worked as a kind of legal assistant, organising the passport applications for the exit visas for the babies.

Joy said she knew all the surrogates well, including our surrogate, Ausa. She said that Ausa was well and that the caesarean – all the babies were born via caesarean – would go ahead as planned the following day. She said she would meet me at the hospital.

Everything seemed calm, clear and in control. So far so good! I reported back to John and then spent the rest of the day exploring downtown Bangkok. I had visited briefly once before, 18 years earlier, on a stopover when I was en route to see my mother in Australia, so I knew that Bangkok was a very westernised city; vibrant, hot and commercial.

In contrast to the squalor, inequality and dirt in Mumbai, Bangkok was squeaky clean, and everyone looked well cared-for. The streets were clean and sunny and there were stalls selling melon, papaya, and pineapple. And there was colour everywhere; the taxis were yellow, green, and bright pink and the tuk-tuks were all kinds of shiny colours, so unlike the battered old rickshaws of the Mumbai suburbs.

But there was another contrast that struck me and made me nostalgic for India. In Mumbai you see a lot of laughter and tears and have a sense that all of human life is happening on those streets, whereas in Bangkok things are strangely clinical and sterile.

Although the official religion of Thailand is Theravada Buddhism, there were huge Santa's on display everywhere and every sign of Christmas, which seemed particularly incongruous in the sizzling heat.

I took the skytrain from close to my apartment to the Phyathai 2 International Hospital in central Bangkok. The skytrain, running on rails set high above the city, is super-modern, clean, fast, and impressive. The trip to the hospital was only five or six stops and the journey took 20 minutes. It allowed me to by-pass the traffic jams and hold-up's that would have made it two or three times as long by taxi or tuk-tuk – the same motorised rickshaws that had been so prolific in Mumbai.

The hospital was smaller than the one in Mumbai but significantly shinier and more modern. Joy met me at reception, next to the ground floor coffee shop, and we headed upstairs to the Neonatal Intensive Care Unit where, through a large glass window, I could see perhaps 12 or 15 babies in cots and lots of nurses, in their pink uniforms.

'This is where your baby will be brought,' Joy explained.

'The nurses do all the post-natal checks here, so that the parents can watch.'

Also waiting outside the NICU were a Dutch couple, Marcella, and Thijs, who were waiting for their twin baby boys, their own biological children, being brought into the world thanks to a surrogate. They were a warm and friendly couple and although they went back to the Netherlands four weeks later, we stayed in touch.

Pacing up and down were another couple, this time British, who were expecting a baby girl.

Charlie and Jian, who was Chinese-British, were excited and chatty, both of them as nervous as the rest of us. Again, I stayed in touch with these two, who made the classic mistake of befriending their surrogate, to the point where she considered herself their baby's mother and they had to slip out of the country without telling her.

But that morning outside the NICU all these decisions lay in the future. We all sat, paced, went for another coffee, and chatted nervously to one another as we waited. For me it meant a lot to be with others in the same boat.

Marcella and Thijs's twins were the first to arrive and they rushed over to stand with their noses glued to the glass window, watching as their babies were cleaned up, checked, wrapped in soft blankets, and placed gently in their cots. After this Marcella and Thijs were invited to get gowned up and go in and meet their children.

By this time, I was so excited and anxious that I could barely breathe. Then a nurse arrived and said that baby Ausa had been delivered and was coming into the NICU. I leaped over to the window as a cot was wheeled into the room and two nurses got to work on the baby. Straining to catch a glimpse all I could see was one small foot one end and a few tufts of dark hair the other.

'He's here,' I mouthed to Charlie and Jian. 'And he's beautiful!' This last was a slight exaggeration, given that I hadn't actually seen his face yet. But I knew he would be.

Half an hour later a nurse came out, a pink gown over her arm, and invited me in. Once I was gowned up, I was led into the NICU and over to our baby's cot.

'Hello,' I whispered. 'I'm your dad.'

I was given a seat beside his cot, and he was lifted into my arms. A tiny 2.6 kilo scrap of humanity – with the lungs of an East End Barrow Boy. He was bawling and he sounded furious, although the nurse said he was just hungry. I looked around – all the other babies were quietly and peacefully sleeping or feeding. But not mine. He was announcing his presence at full volume.

'Were all his checks alright,' I asked? 'Is he healthy?'

'He is perfect,' the nurse said. 'Everything is fine, and you will soon be able to take him home. Does he have a name?'

I was tempted to say Screamer, but I thought better of it.

'Thor,' I told her.

When I knew our baby was going to be a boy, I had remembered my friend Torgeir, the Norwegian I met in India, with his partner Kjertil. Torgeir had been known as Tor and I liked that. I told John about it and suggested we go for the anglicised version, Thor. John had loved it. And how apt to name our noisy boy after the God of Thunder.

After a while I was told they would settle him to sleep. He had probably worn himself out by this point, but even so, it was hard to imagine him quiet for long. I was asked to come back the following morning between eight and nine to feed him. The nurses would then do the intermediate feeds and I could return for the evening feed between five and six.

That afternoon I called John to tell him our son had arrived. 'He's so full of life,' I said. 'Black hair and noisy as hell.'

I called Joy at the clinic. She said she would start the paperwork and recommended a nanny called Nin who she said could help me out once I brought Thor out of hospital.

When I went back to the hospital the next day, I was invited to meet Ausa, the surrogate. Whereas in India it was illegal to meet your surrogate, this was not the case in Thailand, where meeting the surrogate was normal. I said yes, I wanted to thank her and give her a gift, but I was very aware that it would not be a good idea to get to know her. I was taken through to the ward where Ausa was recovering, and I gave her chocolates and flowers and thanked her warmly for what she had done for us. She was looking a little frail, post-caesarean, and her mother and three-year-old daughter were with her. She was very smiley and appreciative, and I was glad to put a face to the name. Later, we sent her some money, to thank her.

While I waited for Thor to come out of hospital I went and bought a car seat, some Pampers nappies and formula to feed him. I had brought some SMA from England with me, but I knew it wouldn't last long so I went and bought some more.

Two days later, on Christmas Day, I brought Thor home. It was sooner than for many other parents because I'd already had experience of looking after babies. How different to after the girls were born when I hadn't had a clue! At this point, I was an old hand at it.

I took him back to the apartment, walking slowly back from the station in the intense heat. Everyone there had known why I was there and when I arrived the receptionist, a friendly Thai girl, hung over Thor, enchanted. I'd requested a cot, which had been placed in my room and I slipped Thor into it. He woke, fed, and went back to sleep. 'This is going to be easy,' I told myself. 'I've got it cracked.'

While he was sleeping, I rang John to tell him Thor was out of hospital and to say Happy Christmas to him and the girls. John told me he'd cooked a full Christmas lunch and I longed to be part of it. I kept thinking about how much Tara loved Brussels sprouts, which was very weird for a tiny girl, given that most adults hated them.

Despite missing the fun back home, I knew that it hadn't been an easy time for John either. Carla, our nanny, had gone back to Slovenia for two weeks the day after I left and after that

John was on his own with the girls and the dogs until the New Year.

John assured me that I was missed and that the girls had loved their presents. After half an hour we said goodbye because the girls had woken from their nap and were yelling. Feeling miserably homesick in the silence of the apartment, I settled down to watch some very strange Thai Christmas show on TV and to wait for our baby boy to wake up.

Chapter 13

Earthquake

For the next four days things went without a glitch. Thor fed and slept well, and I felt like an old hand at the baby business.

I would sometimes take him downstairs where the staff and guests would coo over him and then we'd go up the road to the 7-Eleven shop, where the girls behind the till would also coo over him.

When he was one week old, I took him with me to the clinic to meet Joy, who was sorting out some documentation for me. I had asked her at the hospital about the possibility of a nanny and now she said that she had someone for me. Her friend Nin came to see me later that day and we agreed that she would start the next day. She was in the very early months of a surrogate pregnancy, not yet showing, so while I was concerned that she didn't overdo things, I thought she would probably be especially caring with a new-born baby. She agreed to work from nine until six each day, after which she would go home, and I would do the nights.

Nin appeared to be kind and helpful. But after she began work, when he was eight days old, Thor's behaviour changed. He would sleep quietly all day, but soon after Nin left for the evening he would wake and be terribly restless. He seemed almost to erupt, and he became red-faced, screaming, and distressed. He would scream almost constantly; not just crying but yelling so hard that he was breathless. Suddenly I felt all my parenting skills dissolve, as he and I spent one miserable night after another. I couldn't understand what had gone wrong. I had got him on a four-hourly feeding cycle before Nin came, but now I began feeding him at two-hourly intervals, just to try to soothe and comfort his endless screaming. Even then I had to try to calm him before he would take the bottle. Eventually I was feeding him every hour.

I felt awful. Why couldn't I settle him the way Nin did? What was it that was wrong? Nothing I did seemed to help much. I spent long nights walking him up and down, singing to him, rocking, and soothing him, but neither of us were getting much sleep. It was so different to my experience with Tara and Amritsar who slept well almost from the start.

Each day, exhausted, I would escape the apartment, leaving Thor with Nin and going off to wander the vast, shiny shopping malls or to sit in cafes people-watching. The nights were so awful that I needed to get out of the apartment. And of course, I trusted Nin, she came highly recommended, and she appeared to be the perfect nanny.

After three weeks of Thor's miserable nights, I decided to keep a closer eye on Nin to see what she was doing. Was there some clever trick I could learn from her? Instead of going out I stayed in the apartment, telling her I needed some rest. When Nin was sorting Thor's clothes I went and looked into the cot. I was shocked to find Thor wrapped in thick towels – he even had one round his head. The poor child must have been so hot. This was not the same as Bharti's swaddling in India, where the girls had been wrapped in filmy cotton saris and had certainly not had their heads covered. Thor was almost smothered with towels; this was not for comfort or security; he was clearly being kept artificially hot. Babies who are too hot stay still and quiet, so it was no wonder Nin had him so silent.

I was furious. I took the towels off Thor and then I went and found Nin and tried to explain that this was not acceptable. She didn't speak much English, so it was difficult to get through to her. I had to phone Joy to ask her to tell Nin I couldn't employ her any longer. I had lost trust in her.

It was only after she left that I realised the towels were only a part of the problem. Later that evening, as Thor screamed inconsolably, I knocked over the kitchen bin and when the contents spilled out, I noticed an empty tablet strip. Picking it up I was shocked to see it was a type of sleeping tablet.

I was horrified. What had Nin been doing? Had she been drugging Thor to get him to sleep? He should never have been given any medication without my permission; let alone something he didn't need.

That's when it dawned on me. Nin had been giving Thor a drug and over-heating him, to keep him sedated all day. No wonder the poor child was distressed. I felt awful, realising that this had gone on for three weeks without me realising.

The next day I took the tablet strip to a Boots chemist a couple of streets away. They confirmed that it was a sleeping pill that could be bought over the counter.

I was frantic and angry – and of course I felt guilty too. Poor Thor had been suffering and I hadn't realised what was going on. For the next few days his screaming became even worse, as the drug worked its way out of his system. Nothing soothed him, not even his bottle.

I looked after him on my own for the next week, trying to get him into a better routine and to keep him comfortable. I worried that what Nin had done would have a lasting effect on him. But there was little I could do, other than to wait and see.

There were moments when I thought I was going mad and more than once I phoned John in tears. I did have to walk outside the room a couple of times, closing the door behind me, just to get a minute's relief from the screaming and to keep my sanity. But I never stayed away for long, I knew that if it was hard for me, it was probably harder for him. Inevitably I nicknamed him Bambam, following on from the girls' Booboo and Baabaa.

Given that I had sacked her friend, I couldn't ask Joy to find me another nanny. She was already being a little cool and awkward with me when I rang to ask about the progress of Thor's paperwork. I did some internet research and got in touch with a nanny agency, the Nitiporn, and they said they would send a nanny called Ameena for an interview. She wanted to live-in and could start straight away.

I went down to the hotel lobby to meet Ameena the following day. There was a walkway on the ground floor, with a water feature, at the end of which were a few tables and chairs. The whole reception area was heavily air conditioned and smelled of lemongrass. When I reached the seating area there were two women waiting for me. One was a serene and very beautiful girl and the other a slightly older looking woman. I assumed the younger woman was Ameena and that the older one was there from the Nitiporn Agency to check me out.

I started chatting to the younger one, but she told me that she was from the agency and the other woman was Ameena. I was pleased - after Bharti and Manju I felt rather at home with older, more assertive types. We chatted for a bit, and I learned that Ameena had once been married to a Danish man. They'd had no children and had divorced and after that she felt she didn't want to try marriage again and she had decided to work as a career nanny instead. She was now 55 and hugely experienced, so I offered her the job on the spot.

The interview was on a Friday and Ameena arrived on the following Monday morning with huge suitcase in tow. I was grateful to see her. During the 24 hours before she started, I'd had no sleep at all.

She could speak some English and I knew quite quickly that we would get along just fine. She took over the living room, putting Thor's cot beside her sofa bed, while I had the bedroom, and we shared the ensuite bathroom and the kitchenette. She would knock and come through my room to use the bathroom. Though thankfully, there was a second W.C. besides the kitchenette. Not easy, but we both accepted that was how it was, and we got on with it.

Even Ameena wasn't having an easy time with Thor. He was still wailing ferociously a lot of the time. But she fell in love with him, and probably saved my sanity at the same time. She would walk around with him for hours, singing gently to him. When he woke in the night, she comforted him back to sleep and at last I was able to get some badly needed sleep myself. I was hugely grateful to Ameena, even if she was also occasionally a little smug about her ability to soothe him.

I was under no illusion that it would be a long, tricky business getting Thor's passport and exit visa. I just hoped it wouldn't be anywhere close to the fiasco that happened in India. One truly good thing was that John would be able to come out and visit me at some point. That would make a world of difference.

Even so, the first six weeks were hard. I had no idea how long it was all going to take and, although Thailand was easier than India in terms of mod cons, it was just as lonely.

Bit by bit the documents we needed arrived. The clinic, via Joy, supplied me with a notarised letter, signed by Ausa, giving up any claim to parental responsibility and confirming that she had no objection to Thor returning to the UK with me. Another document confirmed that Ausa was unmarried. This was so important, as Thor could only take my citizenship if the surrogate was unmarried. If Ausa was married the British Government would consider her husband to be the baby's father. In India it had proved very difficult to get this proof, but in Thailand they were aware of the need for it and it was very straightforward. I was relieved and grateful for this. John and I would still need a parental order, making us both full parents to Thor, but at least the first hurdle was out of the way.

Thor's passport application was going through a company called VFS Visa which handled visa applications for a number of countries including Britain, the US and Australia. We put in our application, and I was interviewed by them. It was friendly and well-managed, so different to the cold and austere British Consulate in India. Everything went well and I was told that my application was straightforward, all my documents were correct and there was no reason it should take long.

With all this in place it should have been simple for the Passport Office to issue Thor's passport. But why would they make things easier for us when they could stick to the same old bureaucratic, long-winded, unhelpful way of doing things. I made several visits to the Embassy, but they were pointless, I was told that they couldn't help me, everything was in progress, and I simply had to wait.

I contacted the passport office regularly by email and received replies saying, 'If your passport application is approved, we will notify you in due course'. The word 'if' chilled me. What did they mean IF? Surely it should have been 'when'. I felt I was being treated as a pestering customer, rather than a British national trying to get his son a passport so that we could return home.

In February there was a wonderful distraction from the endless waiting. It was my birthday and John came out to visit me and to meet our son. Kayla and Jamie came out too, grabbing the chance for a break from their own childcare routines. They had left Max and Millie with Kayla's parents, who sent their love, while Tara and Amritsar were with John's sister Sara in Ireland.

It was wonderful to see John, who arrived with a Harrods teddy bear for Thor. I asked Ameena what the Thai for bear was and she said Mi, so the bear became Mimi. It was to become Thor's most beloved toy; he has barely let it go in the years since then.

John was thrilled with Thor and seemed to bond with him immediately. And he liked Ameena. On his first night John and I with Ameena and Thor went out to a seafood restaurant in which we got to choose our live seafood before it was cooked especially for us. With John holding Thor through most of the evening we all ate huge quantities.

One night, just after John arrived, he and I, with Ameena and Thor, went up to the roof terrace of the Marriot building to watch a lunar eclipse together. It was extraordinary, and John, watching the moon and holding Thor, the new son he had just met, had tears in his eyes.

Kayla and Jamie arrived a day after John and we had a wonderful couple of days together, but the week was marred by the fact that I had to disappear in the middle on my first 'visa-run'.

There was a strange complication in Thailand. Even though I had a six-month tourist visa, I was required to leave the country and re-enter every 60 days. By mid-February the 60 days were almost up. Knowing this would happen I had booked a three-night trip to Vietnam to visit Ho Chi Minh City, formerly Saigon.

This meant that I was going to be leaving Thailand in the middle of John's week there. But it also meant that John could be with Thor while I was away, which is why we had planned for the two to coincide.

Vietnam is not a direct neighbour of Thailand, which borders Laos, Cambodia, and Myanmar, but it was a short plane-hop of an hour and a half across Cambodia to get there. I arrived on Monday February 16 and stayed in a grand old hotel, the Majestic, which was built on the banks of the Saigon River. Its French colonial architecture, style and elegance were wonderful. Although I missed John, I decided to enjoy having two days to myself, so I showered and went to the bar for a beer. Extraordinarily, I bumped into an old friend from London, Frank.

We'd got to know one another through work 20 years earlier and hadn't met for most of that time. He was there on business, so we had a drink together and caught up on our news ('five children?' he exclaimed, eyes out on stalks). Later on, we went for another drink in the bar of a nearby hotel. Sitting at a table on the pavement we realised that the 'restaurant' next door was a cover for a brothel; good looking young women, impeccably dressed, went in and out in a constant stream, delivered and picked up on mopeds. Men, all of them Westerners, would also enter through a second door, and they emerged again after 30 minutes. We laughed, as the elderly tourists at tables around us carried on, oblivious.

Frank decided he wanted to see for himself what the delights of this 'restaurant' were like. Off he went, to emerge 30 minutes later with a big smile on his face.

'You look as though you had fun,' I grinned.

'Let's put it this way,' he said. 'I'll never forget tonight for as long as I live.'

The following day was my birthday and I spent it exploring the city. This week was part of the Vietnamese Tết holiday, that marks the Vietnamese New Year and goes on for several days. Tết is short for Tết Nguyên Đán, which means 'Feast of the First Morning of the First Day' and it is the most important festival in the Vietnamese calendar. The date changes every year, based on the cycles of the moon around the earth and the earth around the sun. It is a time when spring is welcomed, a time of feasting and celebrating, of family reunions and ancestor worship. Children are given money and it is considered a good time for a new venture, such as starting a business or moving home. My final evening in Vietnam, Wednesday February 18th, was the Vietnamese New Year's Eve and I spent the evening watching the fireworks across the river, a wonderful display that thrilled the crowds.

I flew back to Thailand on the Thursday. John had loved spending time with Thor and had got to know Ameena too. He liked her and was glad that Thor had someone so trustworthy to look after him with me.

He, Kayla, and Jamie still had three days of their trip left. And with Ameena there for Thor we were able to go out and explore. We had a great and slightly mad time enjoying the fun side of Bangkok. A river cruise, the Royal palace, Khao San Road – the backpacking district, which is full of bars and restaurants – and the ping pong bars of Patpong Road. Kayla loved the ping-pong bars, where you had to buy a bat and you could play. We also ventured into Nana Plaza, the steamier area of Bangkok, where the go-go girls and ladyboys hang out. It was all fun and we enjoyed some great food, a lot of laughter and a view of Bangkok that I hadn't yet seen.

At the end of their week, they all went home, and the loneliness hit me like a wall. I was missing the girls badly, longing to go home, give them a cuddle and introduce their new baby brother. But the wheels of the passport office turned slowly, and all I could do was wait. My only break was an occasional trip to a gay bar that sold cheap beer in the Silom Road area.

On March 25th it was Tara and Amritsar's second birthday. I would have loved to be with them, but I had to settle for listening to their excited shrieks over the phone, as John described them opening their presents and stuffing themselves with cake.

'Miss you Dadda,' they told me over the phone.

'I miss you too girls,' I said. 'More than you can ever know.'

In mid-April, with no passport on the horizon, I needed to make another visa run. This time I decided to keep it simple and go on a specifically organised day trip to Cambodia. Leaving Thor in Ameena's capable hands, I took a four-hour minibus journey to the border, setting off at 4am. This had been organised for the express purpose of renewing visas for expats, so all of us on the bus were in the same situation. When we got to the border we handed in our passports for processing and were taken to a large casino on the Cambodian side of the border. There we were given a buffet breakfast, after which our passports were returned with Cambodian visas and re-entry approval for Thailand. After another four-hour drive I was back at the apartment by four in the afternoon. Job done.

A week after I returned from this brief trip John phoned me. 'Andi?' I could hear the alarm in his voice.

'What is it?'

'Have you seen the news? There's been an earthquake in Nepal, in the Kathmandu area. It looks very serious.'

I rushed to turn on the television news and then sat, transfixed, and horrified, as the story began to emerge.

It was April 25th and Nepal had just been hit by an earthquake which hit 7.8 on the Richter scale. That level of earthquake is absolutely devastating. The epicentre, we would later find out, was in the Gorkha district, to the east of Kathmandu. In total 9000 people were killed and 22,000 injured and quarter of a million lost their homes. Two avalanches were triggered, one on Mount Everest, which killed 21 people, making it the deadliest day in the mountain's history, and another in the Langtang Valley, where 250 people died. The aftershocks went on for many days, as entire villages were flattened, and many ancient buildings and heritage sites were destroyed.

All of this we would discover over the following days, as we watched and waited for news of our surrogate, Sushila, and her pregnancy with our two children.

I had emailed Doron immediately, but of course initially he had no more information than I did. It was several days before he was able to get back to me to say that the surrogates, including Sushila, were fine. They were all living together in a house in Kathmandu, where they were cared for by the clinic. After the earthquake food and supply lines had been disrupted, so things were tough for them, but they were managing.

The Grande City Clinic had been sending us monthly email reports and scans, via Tammuz, and we knew that our babies were doing well. They were due to be born in early July, so by the time of the earthquake Sushila was over six months pregnant. John and I, talking every day about our fears and concerns, could only hope that all would be well.

A few weeks after the earthquake Doron sent an Israeli doctor to Nepal to check the health of the surrogates and their babies. The report he sent back said that all were healthy. And it also revealed that we were expecting a boy and a girl. We were thrilled. Our family would be complete; Amritsar, Tara and Thor would have a brother and a sister to join them.

First, though, I had to get home from Thailand with Thor, and then travel to Nepal. For the next few weeks, I worried constantly – would Thor's passport arrive in time? What if I didn't make it back before the babies were born in Nepal? It was all getting far too close for comfort.

Desperate to get things moving I emailed the British Ambassador to Thailand as well as the Embassy, expecting to receive the same 'we will notify you in due course' message I'd had every other time. But to my surprise, I got an email back from a woman named Sarah Peters in the Foreign and Commonwealth Office (FCO). She said that she would try to help speed things up. I felt encouraged, this seemed like a positive step. I emailed back to thank her and phoned John to let him know. But in the days after her message there was still no news.

Restless and frustrated, I decided that we needed a change of scenery. I booked a riverside apartment close to Sapham Taksin skytrain station, on the other side of Bangkok and Ameena, Thor and I moved in. It had a river view, and it was good to be somewhere different. I took it for two weeks, hoping that by then Thor's passport would arrive and we could go home.

Chapter 14

New Recruit

I opened my eyes. My head hurt. In fact, I was hurting all over. I felt terrible; aching, nauseous and my head felt blurry. What had happened?

The night before Ameena had taken Thor to her parents' house for the weekend, to give me a break. I decided to go to one of the gay clubs, danced, had a few drinks. But that wouldn't leave me feeling so awful. And how had I got home? Why couldn't I remember? What else had happened? It was all a blur.

I turned my head – and couldn't believe my eyes. There was a man lying next to me, a thickset, tattooed man. I was horrified. Had I invited him back to the apartment? I wouldn't have, I didn't do that sort of thing. But here he was.

Awash with guilt and shame, I woke him, hustled him out of the apartment, made a coffee and tried to piece things together. I had been in a good mood, excited at having some time off. I was chatting dancing having a good time. I remembered being offered a joint and I'd had a few puffs. The music was hypnotic, I danced some more, the guy with the joint kept offering it to me so I had a few puffs.

Beyond that I couldn't remember. Had I been given stronger drugs? Had my drink been spiked? Something had happened because I would not have invited a man back to the apartment.

Feeling violently sick and shaking with distress, I went to shower. I scrubbed at my skin with hot water for a long time, miserable and full of self-loathing. How would I ever tell John what had happened? And yet how could I not? We had an open and honest – and faithful – relationship. I suspected that I had been drugged and date raped. But I had no proof and there was nothing I could do.

I mooched around the apartment all day, speaking briefly to John (I wasn't ready to talk about what had happened yet) and wishing I had never gone out. Thankfully Ameena and Thor would be back the next morning. That evening I decided to take no chances, I felt too ill to go out anyway; I would stay in with a bowl of popcorn and a movie. I stuck the popcorn in the microwave and went to have another shower. I still felt sick, miserable, and full of regret.

I stepped out of the shower and smelt burning. I ran through to the living room, where there was a thick cloud of smoke pouring from the kitchen. I rushed through and realised that the microwave was still going. Still groggy, I must have turned it to 20 minutes instead of two.

Thinking that the day couldn't get any worse, I turned it off, opened the door and chucked the blackened ashes of the popcorn in the bin. Then I put the air-conditioning on full blast and opened the French doors into the terrace, hoping to dispel the smoke and the acrid smell of burning.

Minutes later there was a loud knock at the door. I opened it to find my Indian landlord, who lived in the floor above mine, with his nephew, known as Tiger, who was the agent for the apartments. They pushed their way in, both screaming.

I showed them the microwave and explained that it was an accident, and I would clean everything up. 'This was just a small popcorn fire in the microwave,' I said. 'There is no danger, nothing is damaged.'

Tiger looked at me, his eyes narrowed. 'There is bad smell,' he said. 'You ruin apartment.'

'I haven't ruined it,' I said. 'The smell will go, and I will clean up. Please come back in 24 hours, I promise you it will all be as good as new. This is not a big problem, honestly.'

Tiger told me that there was a retired policeman living upstairs. 'We call police,' he said.

I was losing patience. 'Please don't do that, I will sort it all out. Now please go.'

Vowing to return the two of them left, still cursing me.

For the next few hours, I scrubbed and cleaned until the apartment looked perfect and the microwave was gleaming. There was a faint smell, but I was sure it would disappear by the next day. By the time I'd finished I felt exhausted. With no energy for the movie I fell into bed, hoping to put the whole miserable series of events behind me.

In the morning I felt better. The apartment looked fine, and I opened the French windows again to get rid of the last of the smell. I expected the landlord and Tiger to return, but there was no sign of them, and I hoped they had let it go. But at four in the afternoon, there was a pounding on the door.

'Ok, ok,' I muttered, hurrying to open it.

Outside stood a police officer. And behind him I could see there were several more. The landlord had clearly shopped me, but wasn't this rather overdoing it?

In they came and, to my astonishment and dismay, there were sixteen of them, some in uniform and some in plain clothes. Behind them was a small, neatly dressed Thai woman, the supervisor of the apartments. I thought about cracking a joke, 'Hey, is this what you always do after a popcorn fire?' but I looked at their grim faces, shiny badges and holstered guns and thought better of it.

The police started searching the apartment. What were they looking for? I had nothing there other than a few clothes and Thor's baby paraphernalia. Then the supervisor turned to me. 'You have to give your pee now,' she said. That's when the penny dropped. They were looking for drugs. Still stunned by what was going on, I did as I was told.

My urine was tested on the spot. The officer doing it looked up and smiled. 'You come with us now'.

My heart sank. I must have tested positive. I didn't even know what drug was in my system, but clearly, I'd been given something more than a few puffs of weed. It was only later that I would learn it was crystal meth. It must have been slipped into my drink at the club that night.

The police indicated that I had to go with them. Before they led me off the supervisor told me to take my things. The apartment owners wanted me out. I couldn't take Thor and Ameena's things, but I shoved all my stuff into my case and said we would be back for the rest. 'You can pay for all this to go away,' the supervisor hissed as she left. After which I was frog-marched with a policeman either side of me, to a waiting Shogun jeep. three officers got in with me.

As we drove through Bangkok, I had a sense of the unreal. This couldn't be happening; I had done nothing wrong, apart from burning some popcorn. If there were drugs in my system, it was because I was the victim of a crime and yet I was the one in trouble.

When we reached police headquarters, I wasn't handcuffed or put in a cell. Instead, I was left in an interrogation room with a large LED screen at one end, adorned by a huge picture of a cannabis leaf. Was this the drug-squad's idea of a joke?

I wasn't badly treated, in fact they fed me and let me have a cigarette out on the rear fire escape. No-one seemed to speak English, so the apartment supervisor was called in to translate. Through her I made a statement, telling them what I could remember of the previous 48 hours. After which the supervisor and the officers talked together in Thai and various phone calls were made.

Finally, the supervisor came back to me. She told me that I had a choice. I could wait six months for a court date and then go to prison for three months for the consumption of illegal drugs. Or I could be treated for my 'addiction' for 15 days, after which I would be free to go, with no record.

'I am not an addict,' I told her. 'I was drugged.'

'This not important,' she said. 'You are a farang and they want to make example of you.'

A farang was someone from the west. I realised then that there was not a lot of point in explaining that I wasn't an addict.

I couldn't face a six-month wait and then prison.

'Where would I be treated,' I asked her. 'In a hospital?' I pictured somewhere cool and clean and quiet. Two weeks there wouldn't be so bad.

'In the army,' she said.

The army? The Thai Army? Was this what normally happened for a minor drugs offence?

'This is new project,' the supervisor said. 'Army will not be bad; they want you to think they are good. You should be thankful.'

I hoped she was right. Because I definitely was not army material.

She left and I was bundled back into the jeep and driven to the army barracks in Bangkok, but when we arrived it seemed there was nobody there to admit me. I was driven back to the police station.

I put my head in my hands. How had this unfortunate chain of events come about? I blamed myself for moving and for going out and being reckless. I wanted to celebrate a night off, but I wasn't careful enough. At that moment I would have given anything to be settled back in the Marriot apartment with Thor bawling his head off beside me.

Back at the station I was taken into the interrogation room and given a camp bed for the night. Food was brought in from the local 7-Eleven, but I couldn't eat. Two burly officers stayed with me in the room, where I curled up miserably on my narrow bed, and slept fitfully for the next few hours. Every time I woke, fear surged through me. What was I facing? Just how brutal was the Thai army? Visions of all the gruesome war films I'd ever seen raced through my mind. Would I be crawling on my belly through grenade-strewn paddy fields? Or beaten half to death? Or ordered to run 30 miles with a 20-kilo backpack? My over-active imagination was having a field day.

The one thing I was grateful for was that Ameena had Thor; she loved him and would take care of him. I had been with Ameena to her parents' house and had met them and her sisters a couple of times before I agreed to let her take Thor there for the weekend. They were a good family, and I knew that Thor was safe with them. All I needed was to get a message to Ameena to hang onto him. And of course, I needed to tell John what was going on.

I wondered whether my contact at the Embassy, Sarah Peters could help me. I would ask if I could call her.

In the morning I was allowed to call Ameena and arrange to meet her, with Thor, at the apartment to clear out their things. When I saw Thor, I felt close to tears. I just wanted to take him home, and now he had to go back to Ameena's, and I had to go goodness knows where for two whole weeks.

Ameena and I packed all of their things and she promised that Thor would be very safe. As I was led away, she was in tears.

'You be OK Mr Andi,' she said. 'I wait for you with Thor.'

As I was driven away in the jeep, I remembered what the supervisor had said and decided that if there was a chance of paying my way out of this mess it had to be now. I slipped £150 out of my wallet and offered it to the most senior officer. He took one look and said, 'No, this is too late, your paperwork is with the army now.' I put the money away again. That idea was well and truly quashed.

An hour later we arrived at a set of prefab buildings. Inside there was a lot of Thai army material – posters and so on, and seating for around 40 people where there were a number of Thai men. Minutes later two men in suits came to greet the officers and I was handed over to their care.

'Greetings,' one of them said. 'We are very happy that you are here. For some time now, we have wanted a foreigner to participate in our military scheme to rehabilitate offenders. Now you will be the first foreigner joining the Royal Thai Army.'

He looked pleased. It seemed that I was something of a novelty; I only hoped that would be enough to keep me safe and ensure good treatment.

I was asked to sit and wait with the other men. One by one they were called into another room. When my turn came the two men in suits appeared.

They took me into a side room and explained that after 15 days I would be allowed to go home with no criminal record. I agreed to this – what other choice did I have – so I signed the paperwork and they allowed me to call John.

I told him, in brief, what had happened. He was torn between being furious with me and concerned for me. I understood his anger, but the time for recriminations would be later.

'Don't let anyone else know,' I said. I was thinking of my mother, always so supportive but likely to be horrified if she heard.

'Don't worry,' John said. 'I'll tell everyone you're worn out and need some R and R so you're going on a retreat and Thor is visiting Ameena's family.'

I had to laugh. A retreat?

'Thanks John.' I felt tearful. 'I'll call you as soon as I am free.'

I managed one more call before the battery on my phone died. Sarah Peters sounded concerned and said she would try to help. 'We'll see if we can get someone from the Embassy to visit you,' she said. 'Where is your son? Give me the address, he needs to be collected by social services.'

I was shocked. 'No,' I told her. 'He's fine, he's with the person who has looked after him night and day for the past three months. He's safe, I trust her completely.'

Later I learned that she had phoned John and said, untruthfully, that I had given permission for him to give her Ameena's address. Her only concern seemed to be to take Thor into care. Thankfully John refused, he knew that the best place for Thor was with Ameena.

Calls made, I was taken outside with the other men, and we were loaded into several troop-carriers and then driven for several hours up-country. On the journey, as we jolted around in the back of the carrier, I tried to talk to my fellow passengers, but no-one spoke English, although they seemed friendly. As the light was fading, I couldn't see much of the surrounding countryside, but later, on the journey back, I saw that we were close to the River Kwai, made infamous by the epic film about prisoners in World War Two, building a bridge over the river.

It was late evening and very dark by the time the troop-carrier left the main road and went through the gates of the 29th Battalion Infantry.

Outside a large two-storey concrete building we were offloaded. Inside the lighting was dim. We were sat in rows in a large room, youngest at the front, older men behind. The front row was ordered to stand, strip naked and then jog into the shower room next door.

When my row was ordered to do the same, I left my bag, phone and clothes in a heap and took my place in the shower queue. The water was cold, but the shower felt good after the dusty journey. Clean and dry, along with my fellow recruits I was given the standard-issue cadet's white t-shirt and shorts. As I dressed, I could see, through the open window, there were fireflies dancing outside. For a few seconds it was captivating to watch, but a moment later we were marched back to the main room, where we sat, cross-legged, on the floor.

For the next two weeks we underwent boot-camp training. Each group was 18 men and there were groups ahead of us and behind us – some about to leave, others arriving. We spent our days marching in unison and shouting, 'One, two three, four,' in Thai (nuang, song sarm, si). As a child I'd never been an army or a sea cadet or anything even vaguely military, so this was my first, and hopefully last, experience of military drilling and, given that there was no choice anyway, I gave it my all.

Andi Webb

I was older than most of the men. Most were in their twenties, so there had to be some concessions. I refused to run around the field three times every morning or to do bar-lifts, pulling up my bodyweight holding onto a metal bar. I told them I couldn't do it and they said alright. We were all able to work within our limits and there was no punishment if you couldn't do it.

Facilities were basic. No shower but a big communal 'pool'. You were given a toothbrush and a bar of soap. We had to share a single cup which was kept on the water bottle stand. Get in the pool, lather up, clean your teeth and out again. Food was also basic, but edible. Bed was concrete slab with a straw mattress on it. The bed bugs bit badly, but they would blister up and be gone within an hour. I did catch scabies though and had to be treated for it once I got home.

We were, I discovered, in a vast area, carved out of the jungle, and home to many divisions of the army. There were dozens of similar compounds to ours on the same site. There was no running away – you could have run for 50 miles and still be in the camp.

I did my best to bond with my team-mates, but it wasn't easy, given that they spoke no English and I spoke no Thai. We did a lot of nodding and smiling. The only person who spoke English was in the group a week ahead of mine. His father had lived in California for a bit. We managed a few chats before his group was taken back to Bangkok for release. Other than that, I sat and listened to the guys chatting each evening but didn't understand a word.

The officers, one or two of whom spoke a little English, did tell me that there was another farang who they didn't want because he was complaining all the time. They said, 'that man very bad for army'. Goodness knows what they did with him for his two weeks. Clearly, he was side-lined, and I was declared to be the first full westerner to enter the programme. I felt honour-bound to step up and fulfil their expectations.

In our squad there was one ladyboy. The ladyboys, for which Thailand is famous, are men who dress as women so convincingly that it's almost impossible to tell the difference. Or as one definition put it, 'A man with all the attributes of a woman except for the plumbing'. Our ladyboy was very feminine and looked out of place among the men. He was in his forty's, and he ended up doing all the laundry for the squad. He also got it on with one of the other guys and they seemed so in love that it looked all set to continue after they left.

Our commander was called Marjung, and he was alright, although he clearly had over-friendly tendencies. At one point he invited me to sleep in his room to be 'more comfortable'. Alarmed, I thanked him and said I must decline as I felt I should stay with my comrades.

The second week dragged; I was longing to get home. Added to things was the fact that an animal must have died nearby and there were flies everywhere. I had to learn not to react to the flies constantly crawling all over me.

There was an official regiment song we had to chant, and we were all required to learn it. I discovered that if I just shouted the same as everybody else, I could blend in, and it appeared that I was shouting the same thing. All the big cheeses in the squadron would listen to me and laughingly say, 'Good, good'.

At the end of the two weeks, I was fitter and thinner, but other than an itchy case of scabies, no worse off than I had been before the whole escapade. I'd had a lot of time to think to miss my family and to promise myself that I would never take stupid risks again. I couldn't afford to; I was a father of three and that was about to become five.

I was given my things back and driven, with the rest of my troop, back to the prefab site in Bangkok for our graduation ceremony. We duly sang our regiment song, with me proudly word-perfect, after which I lined up with the others to collect our certificates. I've no idea what mine said, but whatever it was I felt I'd earned it.

After the ceremony the commander, Marjung, came over to me, smiling. 'Come, come,' he said, waving me towards the back of the graduation area. I wondered what he wanted. I was keen to get away, check back into the Marriot – oh the joy of a real bed again – and contact Ameena so that she would return with Thor.

Marjung, meanwhile, was beside himself with delight. 'I have arranged for your family to be here,' he said triumphantly, patting my shoulder and pointing.

A moment later I spotted them. Beside some tables in a back area stood Ameena with Thor in a baby sling. And next to her, smiling broadly, was John.

Chapter 15

<u>The Last to Leave</u>

I couldn't believe my eyes. I was stunned, and close to tears.

John hugged me. 'You're looking good,' he said. 'All that marching agreed with you then?'

I laughed. 'Yup, I'm going to miss it. Not to mention the straw mattress and canteen food.'

Ameena was smiling broadly, and she handed Thor to me for a cuddle. He looked so well; I had missed him hugely.

'Thank-you for looking after him Ameena,' I said.

'No problem, Mr Andi,' she smiled. 'Thor is good baby. All family love him. And now you are back safe.'

We took a taxi to the hotel John had booked, which turned out to be the same one the surrogacy clinic had moved to after their premises were shut down. Strangely our apartment was two floors directly above the IVF laboratory where Thor had been conceived.

The hotel was also, as it happened, across the road from the British Embassy and the next morning John said we should go over and see them. I told him there was no point, they weren't going to help. But he insisted we give it a try.

I expected that John would have to go home in a few days' time, and I would continue to wait, with Ameena and Thor, for the passport to come through. It was now only two months until the twins were due in Nepal, so I was worried. Perhaps John was right, it wouldn't hurt to go and make a fuss at the Embassy once more. And I wanted to complain about Sarah Peters' attempt to take Thor into care. John had filled me in on her call to him and we were both upset about it.

Inside the Embassy we were asked to wait and then ushered into a side room where, after a few minutes, a tall, thin young man appeared holding a file.

'Er, Mr Webb, I have your son's passport here.'

I had been all set to create hell about it not being ready. I was, momentarily, stunned into silence.

John was laughing.

'You knew!' I said, accusingly.

'I did,' he grinned.

'I believe your son will actually be the last British surrogate baby to leave Thailand,' the young man said. 'Congratulations.'

We thanked him and took the passport. I told him I wasn't happy about Sarah Peters' behaviour, and he, of course, said he knew nothing about it and we would need to take it up in London. We assured him that we would.

'Can you believe that' I said as we waited to cross the road back to our hotel. 'The girls were the last British surrogate babies to leave India, and now Thor is the last from Thailand.'

'You couldn't make it up,' John said. 'We have to be all kinds of lucky for that to have worked out.'

'If you call sitting around waiting for a total of 13 months lucky,' I said. But he was right; we had come frighteningly close to missing out on having our children at all. Now it was impossible to imagine being without them, so no matter what we had to go through, we were lucky. And we were incredibly lucky, too, that our two babies in Nepal were safe and well. I said a silent prayer that they would be born healthy, and I would be there to be with them and bring them home.

We booked our tickets back to England for the next day. I would only have a few weeks before I needed to leave again, so I was anxious to return as soon as possible.

With everything in place, I called my mother. John had told her I was off having a break, but she hadn't believed him – she knew I wouldn't have gone two weeks without calling her. I stuck to the story though and assured her I was fine.

Ameena's sisters came to say goodbye the following morning – they had grown to love Thor almost as much as Ameena did. We were touched. Their family had stepped in and cared for him when I was in trouble, and we were truly grateful. As for Ameena, she was in tears. I would miss her.

We were at the airport when John received a text from Sarah Peters saying that social services had been alerted and there would be a caseworker wanting to see us back in the UK. John was livid at this malevolent and unnecessary intervention. Far from helping us, the British authorities appeared to have done everything they could to make our lives harder.

On the 13-hour flight home we took turns holding Thor who was, thankfully, asleep for a lot of the flight. Coming back from India we'd taken one baby each. We were sitting a few rows apart, so no-one realised that we were together. I'd started off with Tara, who bawled her head off while Amritsar slept peacefully in John's arms. The woman next to John had said, 'Really, what a noise, why can't that parent control the child'. John had replied, deadpan, 'Actually she's this one's twin'. After that the woman pretended to be asleep for the rest of the flight. After a bit John came over and offered to take Tara while I had a break with Amritsar. Of course, Tara then fell asleep with John while I struggled with a bawling Amritsar!

I couldn't wait to see the girls. Would they remember me? Five months is such a long time when you're so small, I was afraid that I might have become a rather blurry memory.

We headed straight to the flat, where the girls had been while John was away, with John's sister Sara and Carla looking after them. When we arrived back, they were at preschool. John had enrolled them in a preschool in West Kensington, the Monkey Puzzle, to help Carla out in the mornings, so John and I went to collect them together. They saw John first, and came running over, shouting, 'Daddy, Daddy'. They saw me and stopped dead, before jumping up and down shouting, Dadda, Dadda' and hurling themselves at me. I was so happy to see them, both taller and so much more grown-up that it was startling. They were talking – not just random words, rather starting to string words together. It was wonderful to be able to hold small conversations with them.

We took them home to meet their baby brother Thor. They were fascinated by him, taking turns to chat to him, tickle him and hold him – with a little adult assistance – on their laps. Thor tolerated all this with a slightly bemused expression, before falling asleep.

The girls were puzzled about where Thor had come from. 'Are we keeping him?' they asked.

'Yes,' I grinned. 'We definitely are.'

Carla had been a real help to John in looking after the girls, but she was 19 and inexperienced and she had been struggling to cope. This meant she had skimped on quite a few chores and simply stuck to getting through it all. John had told me that by the end she was close to falling apart and I could see that because the flat looked wrecked. The place was filthy, there were jammy forks stuck on the kitchen worktops, grease marks, pawprints and handprints all over what had been clean and recently painted walls. The girl's toys were shoved into one of the chimney breasts and in their room clothes and bedding were all over the place.

John was sheepish. 'Andi, Carla was barely coping. I needed to keep her going, whatever way worked. If it's a mess, well, we'll clean it up. To be honest when I was away, I don't think she even bathed the girls or washed their hair once.' It was John who did bath time with them at weekends and on a Wednesday, no wonder he'd asked his sister to come over this last time.

I knew he was right. The girls were well and happy and that's what mattered. We'd sort it out, repaint the walls, get everything clean and sorted again. Not that there was much chance in the days that followed, because Carla went down with flu almost as soon as I got back. I was up each day by about 6am, got them all ready, set off for preschool with Thor in a sling on my back and the girls in a double-buggy, rushed home with Thor to make beds, hoover, feed him, make lunch, went back to get the girls, and then spent the afternoon with all three of them.

It was full-on because the girls were now cheeky two-year-olds with minds of their own. They would drip milk on each other's heads – their current favourite game – and laugh their heads off. Then Amritsar would make a 'brrrrr brrrrr' noise, like a bird, to get our attention. They hid toys, lay on top of the dogs, squashed food into chairs and generally acted like, well, two-year-olds.

Most of the time I had to smile because they could be hilarious. But I had to impose a bit of discipline too, which meant insisting they get off the dogs, clean up their toys and have their hair washed at bath time.

I was managing all of this on very little sleep because Thor was finding it hard to settle. We put him in a Moses basket, with a musical toy and a small light, but he screamed the place down. We would take him out, soothe and rock him and then put him back and he'd start screaming all over again.

I would end up rocking him in my arms while we listened to very loud opera. After 20 minutes of this he would start to close his eyes, but any slight movements and he would be bolt awake again, so tiptoeing out of the room was essential, otherwise we were back to square one!

In Thailand he had been sleeping with Ameena on a mattress on the floor. He felt warm and safe next to her and he could look around and see the room. I realised that he was probably feeling too isolated and too enclosed in the Moses basket. We ditched it and plonked him in the middle of our bed, between the two of us, where he slept better – John and I got barely any sleep at all. Especially as the dogs had been sleeping on the bed and now, they were turfed off. It was a definite case of overcrowding!

Meanwhile the authorities were on our backs as a result of Sarah Peters' heartless intervention. The Home Office had instigated a case file and as soon as we got back, I was ordered to see a doctor in a Kensington medical centre to make sure that I was psychologically sound and able to look after a child. When I went for the appointment, the doctor just looked embarrassed and said, 'I'm afraid they've made a case, so I must look at you'. I told her it was fine, I understood, and she wrote a report saying I was absolutely sound in every way.

This didn't prevent a visit to the flat from a Hammersmith and Fulham social worker intent on scrutinising our 'family skills'. He looked around and then sat down for a cup of tea and told us that this was his final case before leaving the job. He said he didn't think there was a case here at all and went off to write his report.

It was all over fairly quickly, but I felt incensed. Sarah Peters had not only failed to help, but she had also undermined me by trying to take Thor into care and then opening a case file questioning me as a parent. The fact that I had no criminal record in Thailand – I was never charged, and the offence was expunged when I did the two weeks in the camp – only made her actions more infuriating. I seethed over it, but I knew I had to let it go. I was in the clear and that was all that mattered.

John and I were tense with one another during this time. He wasn't happy that I'd got into trouble, and I felt unsupported by him. We got past it, we'd had 20 years together and we knew how to navigate disagreement. But it was a tough time.

We also had to apply to the family courts for Thor's Parental Order as soon as we got back, because he was coming up to the six months deadline. As with the girls we needed a Parental Order to transfer legal rights from the birth mother to me and John and for this we needed Ausa, our surrogate's acknowledgement of the proceedings and confirmation that she understood the legal implications. The court forms needed to be translated into Thai and a notarised document saying she understood needed to be signed. I asked the clinic to help, but the wheels were proving very slow. And to make matters more complicated, because getting Tara and Amritsar's Parental Orders had been so expensive using lawyers, John decided that we should represent ourselves in Thor's case. The judge, when we got to court, didn't like that at all and the case was knocked back on the basis that we didn't have all the right paperwork.

There was no time to sort it out because I was due to go to Nepal. And with that looming over us, we needed to organise childcare and decide how we were going to live once we had five children.

We were muddling along with the girls it the small box room in the flat, Carla in one bedroom and me and John in the other – with Thor in with us. But clearly the flat was getting too crowded and with two more children it would be impossible. Add to this the thinness of the walls and our concern for our neighbours when one or other child was yelling in the middle of the night and we began to wonder whether we might not be better off using Long River as our base, rather than our weekend home.

It would be tougher on John, who would have to commute, but better in every other way. the schools close-by were good, the dogs and children would have the garden, there was lots of space and there were nice thick walls between us and our neighbours.

A couple of weeks after I got back, preschool ended, and we moved to Long River for the summer holidays – and planned that we would then stay on there the following term. The girls could be enrolled in a local preschool, and we would settle down to life in the country.

John had already got to know our neighbours well during the eight months I was in India, and they were very welcoming towards us and the children.

We decided that now was the time for a full-time nanny, rather than an au pair. Apart from the need for more experience and someone who could work longer hours, John was fed-up with having someone live in. He liked to come home to eat dinner and spend the evening with me and the children, rather than having another adult around to eat, talk and share the TV. As he pointed out, there were two types of au pair, the social ones who stayed out of your hair and partied all night but were then wrecked and useless the next day, or the quiet ones who worked hard but were then hanging around all evening.

Carla was ready to move on, she wanted to stay in London and wasn't keen to move to Long River, and we all knew there was absolutely no way that she could manage Thor as well as the girls, so we parted company amicably. After which we advertised, interviewed together and finally opted for two nannies, Chrissy, and Tamsin. Chrissy was the more experienced of the two did the early shift, starting at 7am and working until the afternoon. Tamsin had been working in the elderly care sector and this was her first nannying job, but we liked her so much we decided to give her a job too. She came in part-time, from when Chrissy left until John got home from work.

We had decided that it would be too hard for the girls, emotionally, if I disappeared for what could potentially be at least another five or six months. We agreed that I would commute from Nepal, spending two weeks there before flying back home for two weeks and so on. For that to work we needed absolutely trustworthy childcare in place in Nepal. Someone I could leave our babies with knowing they would be loved and cared for. Who better than Bharti, the warm and wise nanny who had cared for Tara and Amritsar so lovingly for several months in India!

I called her and asked, cautiously if she would agree to come to Nepal with me to look after our two new babies. She agreed, and said that she could bring a close friend, Rekha from Chandigarh with her to help. I told her I would fly to Mumbai in early July to collect them both and we would fly on to Nepal together.

With that sorted both John and I felt hugely relieved. Bharti would take care of one end and Chrissy and Tamsin the other. So far Chrissy and Tamsin had worked out well and the girls adored them, especially Tamsin. There was just one problem; we had told them I was going to be away, but we hadn't told them there would be two more children arriving. John had felt, and perhaps he was right, that we'd never find a nanny if we told them that in a few months there would be five children under the age of three to look after.

We did, of course, have to tell them the truth eventually, and Chrissy immediately handed in her notice. She said that wasn't what she had signed up for and we couldn't disagree. Tamsin took it in her stride, but she didn't want to work full-time. Instead, she brought a friend along. Helen had a degree and had been working in events management, but she wanted – apparently to her father's despair – to be a nanny. Helen, like Tamsin, was cheerful and outgoing. We gave her the job and she and Tamsin split the day between them. Suddenly we had two bright and lively lipstick-wearing glam-nans. The fact that they were friends helped – they would overlap shifts at lunchtime and the handover was smooth. They loved working together and the girls loved both of them. Everyone was happy.

The reports from Nepal were good and we were told the babies would be born on July 5th. On the first day of July, I kissed John and all three children goodbye and flew the nine and a half hours to Mumbai, where I met up with Bharti and Rekha and we flew on together, another three hours, to Kathmandu. It was a very long day!

I had booked us into a hotel and planned to look for an apartment once I got there. After the earthquake it was hard to know what state the city was in or where we might find a safe place to stay. I needed to be there and see for myself.

The earthquake had devastated the tourist industry on which the country relied. In my hotel the two nannies and I were virtually the only guests. It was a hotel, built in the old Newari style unique to Nepal, with distinctive red brickwork and carved wooden doorways and pillars. It had substantial damage on one side, so the guests were staying on the other side. But apart from a German woman, a French woman, and a North African man (these last two were a couple and at night when their amorous exertions seemed inexhaustible and extremely noisy) there was no-one there.

I became friendly with Suman, the night receptionist. He was local and was always helpful in solving any problems that I had. He introduced me to Sam's bar, popular with expats, trekking guides, and those about to climb Everest (everyone gets to sign their names on the wall) and run by a charming and feisty Austrian woman, Verena. It was in the middle of the tourist area of Thamel, hidden on the upper floor of an old building and was always buzzing and friendly.

I went to check in with the Grande City Clinic and was met by Shrisiti, the Tammuz representative in Nepal. Very glamorous and chatty, she told me that she would help in any way she could.

The next day she took me to meet our surrogate, Susheila, in the clinic. She was very quiet and smiling. I thanked her for what she was doing for us and asked her if the earthquake had frightened her. She nodded, her eyes downcast. 'It was a frightening time,' Shrisiti said. 'We are so thankful that all our surrogates were alright.'

Over the next day or so I started exploring the city. So many buildings had been devastated by the earthquake, it was heart breaking to see. And to make things even more challenging of the local people, we were in the middle of the monsoon and every day the rain bucketed down.

On July 5th, as I waited to go to the hospital for the birth of our son and daughter, I sat in a small courtyard and watched the most extraordinary thunderstorm. Rain pelted down, thunder was crashing overhead, and lightning slashed across the darkened skies.

I hoped it was a positive omen.

Chapter 16

A Family of Seven

As the storm continued to rage, I took a taxi to the clinic, which was in Kantipath, close to the city centre. This clinic had the best medical facilities in Kathmandu and a new wing where the operating theatre and NICU (neonatal intensive care unit) were based.

When I arrived, I was asked to wait in the corridor outside the theatre where the delivery was to take place that afternoon. I paced nervously up and down – a situation I was well used to by that point – and waited anxiously for news.

An hour later a nurse came through the doors of the theatre holding a baby, wrapped in a blanket. 'Your daughter,' she said, placing her carefully in my arms. I gazed down at the tiny, screwed up face nestling inside the folds of the blanket. A moment later the nurse returned. 'And here is your son,' she said, smiling. 'You have two beautiful babies.' She arranged the babies so that I had one lying in each arm.

I hadn't been able to hold the girls until the day after their birth. With Thor it was a couple of hours. But these babies had been born only minutes before. I looked from one tiny face to the other, lost for words.

'Do you have names?' the nurse asked.

'We do. The girl is Aaliyah, and the boy is Caleb'.

'Those are lovely names,' the nurse smiled.

John and I had, as always, discussed names before I left. Caleb was a name we had loved from the start; if our girls had been boys one of them might have been named Caleb. And Aaliyah was a name I had always liked. It means ascended, while Caleb means faithful. Both are Hebrew names and as our babies' arrival was facilitated by an Israeli organisation, Hebrew names seemed appropriate.

A moment later they were whisked off to the NICU to be weighed, washed, and fed and I was asked to return the following morning to help with the 10am feed.

I went back to the hotel and phoned John, feeling emotional and happy. He sounded just as happy the other end. Two more healthy, beautiful children. Our family was complete.

Shrisiti called to congratulate me and she told me that, while Tammuz had a number of births arranged through the clinic, ours were the first British children to be born through surrogacy in Nepal. It seemed that all our children had arrived at significant points in the world's surrogacy timeline.

The following day Bharti came with me to the clinic to meet the newest additions to our family. We both put on blue gowns – arranged by Doron and I was grateful not to be head to foot in pink as I had been in India and Thailand.

Bharti fed one baby while I fed the other, and then we swapped halfway through. After that I was invited to return twice a day for feeds. I sometimes went alone, sometimes with Bharti and Rekha.

Both babies were healthy and feeding well. They would soon be ready to leave the clinic, but I asked the doctor in charge, Dr Sanjay, if they could remain for a few more days, until I had found a suitable apartment. He was quite happy to keep them there.

While I was going to and from the clinic, I got to know several other parents of surrogate babies. Another British couple Chris and Nitesh had a son, Manny, born a week after Aaliyah and Caleb. We became good friends, and I got to know a few Australian couples too, all of them visiting their babies in the NICU.

After the morning feed each day, I went out exploring the city and hoping to find an apartment that would be earthquake-proof, clean and safe. I wandered around Thamel, the main tourist section of the city, thinking that it would be my best bet for an apartment. Not that there were any tourists there at this stage, the only foreigners about were a few aid workers. The earthquake and the monsoon had put paid to tourism, for a while at least. At that time of year there were times when rain swamped the streets of the city, turning them into fast-flowing rivers you had to wade through or skip around.

It was in Thamel that I met a man named Gauri and his wife Meera. He told me that he had no apartments in Thamel, but he had an apartment block in a neighbouring area called Lazimpat. I went to meet him there the next day. The entire block was brand new and had survived the earlier earthquake without so much as a crack in the ceilings. That was good enough for me; I agreed to take an apartment on the fourth floor, resigned to the exorbitant price he was charging me as a foreigner.

When I told Bharti and Rekha they weren't at all sure about it. Many of the local people would never live above the second floor in an area so vulnerable to earthquakes. But Gauri had convinced me, and I reassured the nannies that all would be well.

We moved in a week after the babies were born and brought them home to the apartment the next day. There was a small lift in the block but Bharti and Rekha were both nervous about using it, fearful of being trapped if there was another quake. They insisted on walking up the stairs, but after a couple of days spent trudging up and down, they gave in and took the lift.

The apartment was well-furnished and there were two bedrooms, one for the nannies and babies and one for me. With Bharti and Rekha on the scene, swaddling them in soft saris and taking turns night and day, settling the babies in was fairly easy. Neither was a screamer, like Thor, and the nannies soon got them into a routine. Bharti would sing her vintage Bollywood songs and, just as Tara and Amritsar had, Aaliyah and Caleb loved it.

Rekha was a similar age to Bharti and was also a strong and good-hearted woman. I felt confident that if Bharti had to go home for health reasons, Rekha would be totally trustworthy.

Our biggest problem was supplies. Finding baby formula and nappies was difficult; I had to spend a lot of time trawling the city for whatever could be had. I planned to bring as much as I could from England when I went back each time.

Once again, I visited the British Embassy, hoping to register the twins' birth. I was told that they did not register births abroad anymore. After discussing the way forward with John and Shritisi we agreed the twins needed to become British citizens before they could get passports. This was because with the girls and Thor we were able to prove British citizenship by descent, because their surrogates were not married. But in this case, we had a problem – we could not prove that Sushila was unmarried. I had been told that she was unwed, but later I learned that actually she was married. That was a real problem, because under British law her husband was the babies' father. We needed to apply for citizenship for them directly with the Home Office. This was going to involve gathering together a lot of paperwork, which would take several weeks, even with help from Shrisiti.

After three weeks, with the nannies and babies settled in the apartment, I went back to England for two weeks. I left Bharti and Rekha with enough money for all their needs, plus some for emergencies, and promised I would phone every day.

I had missed John, the girls and Thor so much; it was wonderful to see them. Our British nannies, Tamsin, and Helen were managing the routine well and the children seemed settled and happy. Both Tara and Amritsar were starting to talk by this time. The nannies had introduced them to Disney's Anna and Elsa and the girls' rendition of 'Let it Go' was impressive. I used to tease them by calling the characters Annie and Elsie and the girls would shriek with laughter and say, 'No Dadda, it's Anna and Elsa'. 'Ok,' I'd say. 'I've got it, Annie and Elsie'. Cue more shrieks.

The pattern was set for the next few months. I would spend two weeks in Nepal, missing everyone at home and worrying about them, and then two weeks in England, missing Aaliyah and Caleb and worrying about them instead. The flights were over 11 hours each time, with a time adjustment of almost six hours, so my body clock was constantly all over the place and I began to feel I'd be grateful never to see the inside of another plane again. But it was the best compromise we could find in the circumstances, and I knew that, eventually, it would come to an end.

Adding to my dazed state was the lack of sleep in Nepal. Local packs of street dogs would bark all night long, defending their territory from the pack down the road and the racket meant I often got very little sleep.

Not so with Aaliyah and Caleb, who were very content with Bharti and Rekha, although Aaliyah, like Thor, had become a bit of a screamer, while Caleb was much more chilled-out. I'd given them the nicknames Beebee, for Aliyah and Bobo for Caleb. We bought them socks with pictures of mushrooms on them from one of the few shops still open in the semi-derelict Kathmandu shopping mall. The socks were for two-year-olds, so they were more like tights on our two, but they were perfect for the cool evenings. They'd lie side by side, waving their small mushroom-clad legs around to the sound of old Bollywood films playing on the TV.

By the end of August all our documentation, including an affidavit signed by Sushila saying that she wanted no parental responsibility for the children, was submitted to the Home Office. After that it was a question of waiting and hoping.

Days later, in early September the Nepali government decided to ban commercial surrogacy. For some time, there had been bad press, claiming that foreign companies were making money out of it and that nothing was coming to Nepal. Not strictly true, as many businesses in Nepal did benefit – not least the hospital, the landlords, the clinic support staff and many nannies. But it was also true that most, if not all, of the surrogates were Indian. Nepali women were forbidden to become surrogates and so inevitably Nepali attitudes towards surrogacy were becoming very negative. Once again, we seemed to have got in just under the radar.

As the monsoon ended the tourist trade had begun to pick up again. I enjoyed walking around Thamel, seeing old hippies on nostalgia trips and new hippy wannabees drifting around in their brightly coloured beads. They were in stark contrast to the serious trekkers, marching around with their backpacks and walking boots. I tended to look laid back and so more like the hippies than the backpackers, which meant I was targeted by the many pushy drug-dealers trying to hawk their wares. The days in which the Beatles stayed at the Kathmandu Guest House, smoking dope and selling their message of peace and love were gone; the hawkers now were selling seriously hard drugs. I avoided them like the plague, cursing the fact that after my experience in Thailand I had managed to end up in one of the most drug-riddled cities in the world.

As I had in India and Thailand, I measured our progress by the moon, sitting outside on our fourth-floor balcony with a glass of wine and looking at its comforting glow, especially when it was full. I would think about John, Tara, Amritsar and Thor all under that same moon, half a world away from me and their brother and sister. The moon always gave me comfort, it was a reminder of the continuity of life and a connection to home.

My contemplation of the moon was abruptly interrupted, each evening by the shrill cries of ravens, flying en masse to roost in the palace gardens across the city. The sky would fill with their flapping black wings, it reminded me of the scene in the Wizard of Oz when the sinister winged monkeys flew cackling across the sky. The sheer number of ravens was astonishing; they would appear from all around us, all flying in the same direction.

One morning not long after I'd woken, I was sitting on my bed when it jolted under me. A moment later there was a cracking sound, followed by screams and the sound of the local dogs barking from the streets four stories below us.

Bharti appeared at the door looking frightened. 'Mr Andi, earthquake, we take babies downstairs.'

Another earthquake.

I leaped to my feet and headed straight down the stairs with Bharti and Rekha each carrying one of the babies. My heart was pounding. How bad was this going to be? What was the best way to keep the babies safe? Would Gauri's earthquake-proof building hold up?

Downstairs the nannies sheltered in the hallway while I talked to Raj, the apartment manager, who sat in the building's reception area. Raj, always friendly and helpful, told us to stay where we were while he tried to get more information.

We spent a tense few hours, afraid to go back upstairs, but eventually things seemed to have calmed down with no further shocks. We went cautiously back upstairs, but that night Bharti and Rekha insisted on sleeping in the downstairs entrance hallway with the babies and Raj was quite happy to let them. I decided to sleep upstairs – if I didn't, I'd never get them to come back up there.

I phoned John, who was alarmed but said there was nothing about it on the news. It may not have been big enough to attract international attention, but it was very real and very frightening. I learned later that it measured 5.6 on the Richter scale which was definitely not insignificant.

After another night downstairs the nannies came back up, reassured by the fact that there had been no further tremors or aftershocks and the building was still sound. I was relieved, I had been afraid that they might have wanted to flee the country and return to India. But they stayed stoically at their posts, caring for Aaliyah and Caleb, despite their obvious fear. I was deeply grateful.

After the earthquake my friend Chris went back to the British Embassy to try to get emergency travel documents (ETD) for his baby Manny. Chris and his partner Nitesh had tried the Embassy several times already, in the hope of getting help with Manny's passport application. They usually spoke to a woman named Bipasha, who I had also dealt with. Chris had nicknamed her Bips. She was not unfriendly, but nonetheless the response was always the same, like me they had been politely told to go away every time they had been there.

After a few weeks Nitesh had returned to his job in the UK, leaving Chris and Manny in a small one-bed apartment not far from where we were living. Now, despite the earthquake,

Chris was told that an ETD could not be issued. He told me about it, glumly, over a coffee later that day. I was not in the least surprised. I told him that the embassies in all the countries I had been to, had shared a common bond in being equally unhelpful.

However, to our delight, the babies' British citizenship was granted by the Home Office in September. This was a major hurdle crossed. We now had to apply for their passports, which we were told would take up to twelve more weeks.

A few days later I went back to England for my fortnight there. The weather was balmy and mellow, as it often is in early autumn. John and I had put Tara, Amritsar and Thor to bed and were sitting on the terrace outside, enjoying a glass of wine when my phone went.

It was my older brother Paul, in Australia. He told me that mum was gravely ill. She had been found collapsed at home and taken to hospital where tests showed that she had an internal hernia that had twisted her stomach. Although it was a condition that was operable, the doctors believed she might have been unconscious for up to 24 hours before she was found and by that time her system was shutting down. All they could do was to make her comfortable.

This had come out of the blue. Mum was 79 and in reasonably good health, still active and still calling me every week for a chat. She had given me such a lot of support and she had been so happy to know that she had five grandchildren. It was impossible to take in the news that she was so ill.

When Tara and Amritsar were 14 months old Mum had come to stay with us. She absolutely adored the girls; I had taken pictures of them with her that she treasured. I had hoped she would come again when I got home with Aaliyah and Caleb. Now it was heart breaking to realise that she would never make that trip and would not meet her three youngest grandchildren.

A day later, on September 19th, Paul called to say that Mum had died. I felt heartbroken. It would take time to accept that she was gone; the suddenness of it meant there had been no time to get used to the idea. I was grateful, at least, that she had been well almost to the last and not had to go through a long illness.

John and I sat and talked about her for a long time that evening, remembering her with warmth and affection. I had loved her very much.

Mum's funeral was arranged for October 5th, after my next stint in Nepal. I flew out to Australia and back again very briefly and said my goodbye to her. After her divorce from my dad Mum had reverted to her grandmother's maiden name. She didn't want her own maiden name, since she shared it with her younger sister, who had gone off with dad. Her name became Jean Evelin Paradise. The surname, as she liked to point out, with great pride, was derived from the French Huguenot name Paradiso.

Back in Nepal life was becoming complicated and expensive. On September 23, Nepal's key trading route with

India had been blockaded. Nepal blamed India for this, but India insisted it was the minority Nepalese Madhesi community causing the trouble and demanding more rights. This left Nepal in a very vulnerable position, since it borders India on three sides (the fourth side borders with China) and is reliant on goods coming over from India. As the days passed it became clear that India was behind the blockade, since all the trade routes appeared to be blocked, not just those where the Madhesi were demonstrating. The usual 300 fuel lorries crossing the border dwindled to a handful, resulting in a serious shortage of fuel and a thriving black market. There were also shortages of many other goods, including cooking gas and medicines. The fuel shortage meant that taxis began to charge many times the normal price.

At one point I was charged £70 for the trip to the airport that used to cost £10. I decided I would rather walk the 15 kilometres with my suitcase, than pay such a crazy price, but when I spoke to John he said, 'Andi – pay the £70'. The voice of reason.

I'd had a nightmare time trying to find two car seats in which to transport the babies. I got one, but that was it – no second car seat anywhere.

When I told John he said, 'Are you telling me there is only one car seat in the whole of Kathmandu?'

Having searched high and low for days, at this point I was terse. 'Yes. It would seem that way,' I told him. 'I know it's hard to believe.'

The apartment we were in was expensive and the cost of our stay was escalating alarmingly. So reluctantly I moved us out and into a cheaper apartment five minutes away. This one was not nearly as nice, but to Bharti and Rekha's approval, it was on the ground floor with its own private entrance.

Unfortunately, the new landlord had a very nosey female cousin who lived on the top floor, an unpleasant woman, who would say to the nannies, 'Whose babies? Where is the mama?'

Bharti told her to mind her own business, but she began to hound us. I went to talk to the landlord, but he also said, 'Where's the mama?' I told him she was in the UK, and he reluctantly accepted this. But the woman on the top floor did not. Things culminated in what I called the witch hunt – this nasty woman organised a group of her friends and neighbours and came around to our flat, where they pushed their way in and then began screaming, 'The babies are not yours,' and trying to take them out of the nannies' arms. Poor Bharti was in tears and Rekha was shaking like a leaf.

I eventually managed to push the intruders back out of the door, shouting, 'Get out, this is my apartment, these are my children, and you are not welcome.'

After they left, still shouting at us, we locked the door and drew the curtains. The babies were crying, the nannies were distressed, and I felt very worried. Clearly, we couldn't stay there. We waited until dark, packed our things and left. With nowhere else to go I had begged shelter from my friend Chris, who welcomed us into his tiny apartment, where we all slept on the floor.

The next day we checked into a hotel, and I contacted Gauri and asked whether we could return to the Lazimpat apartment. He welcomed us with open arms – and a hefty bill. But it was worth it to feel safe again after a truly unpleasant experience that left us all very shaken.

We moved back to the Lazimpat apartment in mid-November, by which time, with no passports for the babies in sight, I was facing a problem with my Nepalese visa. When I first arrived in Nepal, I was given a visa for 90 days. This had been extended in September by a further 60 days, but it was now about to expire. And visitors to Nepal could only be given a visa for a maximum of 150 days in any one year, which meant that mine could not be renewed until January 1st.

I couldn't leave Bharti and Rekha with the babies for six weeks so in desperation I went back to the British Embassy. They had never shown the slightest interest in helping me, but would they allow my British children to be left alone for all that time?

To my astonishment, they listened to me. 'We will contact our colleagues in London and see if they can help speed up the passport applications for your children,' Bips told me. I thanked her and went home to wait.

With two days to go before my visa expired, I was told to go to the UK VFS Global offices, on the other side of Kathmandu. I arrived, nannies and babies in tow and was interviewed over the phone by the head of UK overseas passport applications, in Delhi. He told me that the passports would be processed and with me in seven days. But while this was a very positive development, it still didn't help my visa problem. I had to leave the country two days later and still wouldn't be able to return for the babies until January.

Reluctantly I paid the rent to January 4th, packed my things and left Aaliyah and Caleb with Bharti and Rekha, who promised to look after them. On the plane home I fretted and worried. Surely there was something I could do.

It was Kayla who came up with the answer. I had called to tell her what was going on and she suggested I apply for a second passport and get a new 30-day Nepali visa on that. I did a bit of research – you could get a second passport for business reasons, but not on compassionate grounds. OK, if that's what it took...

I phoned the passport office in London and made an appointment for the next morning. When I got to the counter a fresh-faced clerk asked if he could help.

'I represent a firm of chartered accountants in the city of London,' I said, hoping I was exuding confidence. 'The firm has just merged with a company in Riyadh, Saudi Arabia and I need to fly out there on Wednesday to meet the new operations manager and then travel on to Israel to meet with two of our Israeli clients to let them know that our new owners would prefer them to make alternative arrangements. As you know, the

Israelis will not give entry to someone who has just visited an Arab country, so I need a second passport.'

'Ah, absolutely Mr Webb, we understand,' said the clerk.

After a brief chat he asked me to return at five to collect my new passport. The following day, new passport in hand, I headed to the Nepali Embassy near Hyde Park to request a 30-day visa. I was alarmed to find that the man at the counter was the same one who had previously granted my 90-day visa, but luckily, without a flicker of recognition, he gave me the visa.

That afternoon I went back to Long River and called Bharti to say that I would be able to take the children home as soon as their passports arrived. Which they did within days, along with all the documents needed for their exit visas.

John and I flew together to Kathmandu on December 15th. With three children to look after at home, we had agreed that he should wait to come out until the return journey, when I would need his help managing the two babies on the journey home.

As with our other three, John was entranced by Aaliyah and Caleb and he bonded with them immediately, cuddling one on each knee, as we sat in the apartment.

After meeting with Shrisiti from Tammuz the next day, we went to the department of immigration. There was a lengthy process which involved the signatures of eight separate immigration officers, but finally we were issued with exit visas in Aaliyah and Caleb's passports.

Before leaving Kathmandu, I took John to Sam's Bar, where the Austrian woman who ran it, knowing I was not a tourist and had been in the city for months, generously plied with free drinks all night.

On December 18 we said a warm and grateful goodbye to Bharti and Rekha, who were returning to Mumbai on a flight later the same day.

We were flying with Qatar Airlines via Doha and when we arrived at check-in, I was told that my flight, and Aaliyah's, had been cancelled. It was due to a mix-up, but we spent a very tense hour and a half persuading them that it was their mistake. Eventually they allowed up to board, at the 11th hour.

On the first leg the cabin crew gave us eight seats between us so that we could put a baby to sleep beside each of us. As we took off and I watched Kathmandu become a postage stamp beneath the window, I breathed a long sigh of relief.

We were going home.

Postscript

Eighteen Moons

Le Rouret, a small village near Grasse on the Cote d'Azur, August 2018.

The children are now aged between three and five and we're on holiday. The night we arrived at the villa, July 27th, there was a lunar eclipse. The little ones were sleeping soundly as John, and I toasted the large, wondrously red moon with our glasses of chilled Rosé and reminisced about the last red moon we saw together. It was in Bangkok, Thailand, when Thor was just a couple of months old, and it was equally stunning. The moon blossoms every 28 days and wherever one might be in the world it's always there, a constant reminder of home.

It has been an extraordinary journey over the last five years.

It took us three and a half years to fulfil our dream of a family and during that time eighteen full moons passed while I remained in India, Thailand, and Nepal, waiting to bring our children home. As I waited the moon was so often my comfort and companion. I would sit and look up at it and think of home and trust that all would be well, especially during those times when I was afraid, we might never make it. Of course, not making it could never have been an option – our children had arrived and, no matter what it took, they were coming home.

But there were moments when I wasn't sure how we would manage it.

When we finally arrived back with Aaliyah and Caleb in December 2015, our journey over and our family together at last, it brought with it a wonderful sense of completion. I had, at times, been through hell – frightened, alone and facing hostility, prejudice, and obfuscation. But I'd also found friendship, kindness and support and it was those things, from wonderful people like Bharti and Kayla, that I would always remember.

We arrived back in the UK to a joyous reunion with Tara, Amritsar, and Thor – and of course our beloved Remus and Gracie.

All of them were excited about the new arrivals, especially the girls, who ran between Aaliyah and Caleb, stroking their cheeks and waving toys under their noses. Aaliyah and Caleb, almost six months old, must have been confused by the appearance of all these other children. But they flapped their arms up and down, gave gummy smiles, and joined in the general racket as they sat, propped up by cushions, in the middle of the living room.

A couple of days later we celebrated Thor's first birthday – with cake liberally smeared over all five faces – and hard on its heels came Christmas. John's family arrived from Ireland and the air was full of the scent of mulled wine and merriment.

John's mother did ask us, a touch nervously, if we had enough children now and were going to stop. We promised her we were. She adores the children and recently told us, when we went to stay with her, that they're the best behaved of all her 17 grandchildren (including step grandchildren). Clearly, she was making this observation on one of the children's better days!

As 2016 arrived we settled into life as a family. It took some adjusting; we had five children under the age of three which, when I think back on it, was quite a handful. At the time we just got on with it, life so busy that there was little time to stop and reflect. And having gone through so much to have a family, no matter how trying things could be, our overwhelming feeling was gratitude. We had five adorable, healthy, and happy children. How lucky is that?

Today, in mid-2018, we're old hands at managing our brood. John, who commutes to London during the week, makes up for what he misses at weekends and in the early mornings and evenings. He's definitely the pushover dad, the one who always gives in and gives every child a piggyback up the stairs to bed, while I'm tough dad, insisting they walk up and refusing all negotiation on that.

I can't get too pleased with myself though, John says the dogs do to me what the kids do to him – that is, totally disobey. If John says, 'Dogs, bed!' they will go to bed, but if I say it, they will just look at me as if to say, 'Why would we do that?'

I am at home with the children, so I have to be tougher, or we'd never get to school or preschool or get anything done.

We have a nanny, Sindy, who works a morning and afternoon split shift, with a break in the middle of the day. She is firm and kind and the children love her.

Ah, the children. Those adorable babies are growing up so fast. At five years old Tara and Amritsar are now at school and loving it.

Amritsar is analytical and considerate; she likes to think things over. She can also be miss prim; they used to all go in the bath together, but now she prefers to have hers on her own.

Tara is far more boisterous; she piles in with the others and loves to show off. I've got those two down for a lawyer and an actress.

Thor is full of personality. Even at two he would have a conversation with you and express an opinion in a way that was rare at such an age. He is cheeky, funny, and determined and he will always push the boundaries. Aware that he alone is not a twin, he makes up for it in high-velocity energy. Mimi is still his best bear, although he is now one of ten teddies that he is deeply attached to.

Aaliyah can be a little minx, strong willed and obstinate. She's good at letting us know – loudly – what she wants. I love her determination. In the pool on holiday, she has been fearless.

All of them are learning to swim and at this point we have

four wearing armbands – only Aaliyah is swimming solo with just her life vest for buoyancy.

As for Caleb, he's Mr Laid Back. He was slow to talk, mainly because Tara would always jump in and interpret for him, telling us what he wanted. As one of the two youngest of the bunch he will often wait for the others to sort out his problems and bring him what he wants.

At home all the children are up by 6.30am (often earlier) and by nine the girls are in school and the three youngest in preschool. Thor, Caleb, and Aaliyah come home for lunch and their nap, while Tara and Amritsar do a full school day. After supper and bath, they're all in bed by 6.30pm and that's when the adult part of the day should start, except that they often don't go to sleep until later. If John goes up to tell them to settle down, they just carry on screaming, which means it's up to 'bad cop' dad to finally quieten things down for the night.

At the weekends, with no school and no Sindy, the routine is more flexible. We aim to have fun as a family at the weekends, with games in the garden and outings. We skip bath time on a Saturday and John does their Sunday night bath, splashing about with them while I make supper.

Speaking of food, they eat huge amounts for such small people. We get through a packet of cornflakes a day. What will they be getting through when they're teenagers? We try not to think about that quite yet.

Do they run rings around us? I like to think not, but they can be scamps. One day recently when John collected Thor, Aaliyah, and Caleb from preschool he brought them home and then, shutting the front door, went back to the car for the bags, planning to be 30 seconds at most. But he got back to the front door to find it firmly bolted. Caleb had been playing with the very long brass front door bolt that went into the floor. Horrified, John called Thor through the letter box, but the children had all runaway.

After about 10 minutes of futile calling, John decided he'd have to break the window of the downstairs loo to get back in. Leaving the loo strewn with glass, he rushed through the house to see where the children were.

Thor was at the bottom of the stairs screaming, 'Aaliyah has covered me with shampoo...' She had got a new bottle of washing up liquid from the store cupboard and upended it over Thor and Caleb, the kitchen floor, the dining room floor, and the stairs.

John was tempted to laugh at the sight of the boys, with gloop all over their heads, but they all needed lunch, so he sat them at the table, threw some sandwiches together and then started to clean up the mess. Needless to say, it took some time, and the store cupboard is now locked!

When they're in trouble we have the 'thinking chair' where they're asked to take time out and sit for a bit. But whenever one of them is in trouble, they tend to side together and stick up for one another. Aaliyah went through a rather prolonged biting phase and one day when she had sunk her teeth into Thor's arm, she was told to go to the thinking chair, which is in the dining room.

The rest of us were in the living room when Thor got up and went through to where Aaliyah was. I tip-toed after them.

'Are you sorry?' he asked her.

'Yes, Thor, I'm sorry,' she replied.

'OK, well you can get down now,' he said, and he brought her back into the living room.

While family life is full-on and John and I love being parents, it was not until the summer of 2018 that we gained full parental rights over Aaliyah and Caleb.

We had applied for the Parental Orders for these two and Thor at the same time. As the POs for the girls had cost thousands in legal fees, we decided to self-represent and it should have been straightforward, but like so much else along the way, it wasn't. The judge didn't like us doing it ourselves and she knocked the case back a total of 13 times.

We finally got Thor's PO late in 2017, but not before I'd gone out to Thailand to see Ausa, the surrogate, to get her to fill in the correct forms. Sushila, Caleb and Aaliyah's surrogate, had vanished. It took a long time before we traced her, not through Tammuz but through the hospital. Since she was married both she and her husband had to sign the disclaimer forms. Finally, everything was in place and on our fourth court appearance we got the little ones' POs in July 2018, just after their third birthday.

That was a day for celebration. We were, at last, full, legal parents to all five of our children.

What a story it had been. When we first talked about having children and opted for commercial surrogacy, we had no idea what lay ahead. Optimistic and unaware of the potential pitfalls, we imagined it all being straightforward. Instead, it was a venture that grabbed our lives by the feet, turned them upside down and shook them. Nothing would ever be quite the same again. But would we change it? Not for anything. We have five wonderful children and beside that everything else fades into insignificance.

Our dogs, Remus, and Gracie are still with us too. Remus is 10 now but still behaves like an unruly puppy. The children adore them, and they adore the children. With all seven of them on the loose it's mayhem.

One day we will tell the children the stories about how they came to us. They are truly international children born of cooperation between countries and people. Aaliyah and Caleb's birth involved a South African egg donor, fertilisation in Thailand, the embryos travelling to Nepal and then being carried by an Indian woman.

As John says, they will have plenty of places to go and explore when we pack them all off on their gap years.

Well, my final words on our experience of 'Family Planning' as I finish this memoir, sitting here in the blazing sun of Provence. Our friend Liza has just arrived, John's family are joining us next week and I can hardly hear my own thoughts over the children's yells for ice-cream. My thoughts turn to my mother. Just as the moon has been a constant, she is always in my thoughts.

I love you Mum. This story and its future blossom is dedicated to you – Rest in Peace.